Praise for *The Joy of Burnout*

'Come on! Admit it! You know what it is like to have
a sense of being worn out, exhausted, spent, numb, dead, cut off,
disconnected—burn out—either a little bit or big time. This rich
volume is not another chant of "Think this way; you'll feel better."
This rich volume is a way to use that sense of being burnt out
as a launching pad, a doorway into a new sense of joy, vibrancy,
aliveness, passion, excitement. Are you ready to begin?'

—Alvin R. Mahrer, PhD, Professor Emeritus,
University of Ottawa, Canada

'In this inspiring, lovely book, Dina Glouberman collects the
stresses of modern life and the collapse of hope into one word:
Burnout. Describing many life quests, including her own, she
brings a poet's voice and sensibility to the task of helping
people discover radical healing, joy
and their "soul community".'

—Lynn Hoffman, author of *Foundations of Family Therapy*
and *Family Therapy: An Intimate History*

'Imagework pioneer, Dina Glouberman, has written about burnout
with gifted, powerful prose that crackles with intelligence, honesty,
insight and clarity. This is a woman whose compassionate, level
gaze gets the big picture, while never losing sight of the subtle,
paradoxical, aggravating details that make up a real life. Her
approach to healing reflects both heartfelt genuineness
and sophisticated wisdom. An absolute joy to read!'

—Belleruth Naparstek, author of *Your Sixth Sense*
and *Staying Well with Guided Imagery*

The Joy
of Burnout

Dr. Dina Glouberman

The Joy
of Burnout

How the End of the World
Can Be a New Beginning

Also by Dr. Dina Glouberman
Life Choices, Life Changes

Inner Ocean Publishing, Inc.
P.O. Box 1239
Makawao, Maui, HI 96768-1239

Originally published by Hodder and Stoughton, 2002

Excerpt from "East Coker" taken from *Collected Poems 1909–1962* by T. S. Eliot, courtesy of Faber and Faber Ltd.

Cover illustration: Linda Bronson/Artville
Author photograph: Mark Rawley
Cover design: Bill Greaves
Compositor: Debra Lordan
Typeset in Berling by Hewer Text Ltd, Edinburgh

Publisher Cataloging-in-Publication Data

Glouberman, Dina.
    The joy of burnout : how the end of the world can be a new
    beginning / Dina Glouberman.—Makawao, HI : Inner Ocean, 2003, c2002.

        p. ; cm.

    Originally published: The joy of burnout : how the end of the world
    can be a new beginning. London : Hodder and Stoughton, 2000.

    Includes bibliographical references.
    ISBN 1-930722-20-6
        1. Burn out (Psychology) 2. Self-actualization (Psychology) 3. Work—
Psychological aspects. 4. Job stress. I. Title.

BF481 .G56 2003
158.7/23–dc21   0310 CIP

Printed in Canada by Transcontinental
Distributed by Publishers Group West

9 8 7 6 5 4 3 2 1

To Ari and Chloe

Acknowledgements

It would be much too embarrassing to burn out while writing a book on burnout. The days of 'those who can't do, teach' are over. All the advice in this book has been tested daily as I've pulled myself back from the brink and put myself on course, breathing and finding my joy while writing for a deadline. Happily, it works.

One of the important aspects of what I call 'Radical Healing' is opening up to a soul community. I take this opportunity to thank my own soul community for holding me, supporting me and pushing me to refine my thinking and my writing.

Without Ilene Sawka and our early discussions on burnout, this book would not have been conceived. Lois Graessle read every draft of this book from the moment of its inception, and spent hours and days to support me throughout and help me to grow it. Hermione Elliott helped birth the book, editing with me during those crucial last days.

Rupert Sheldrake, Piero Ferruci and Bruce Lloyd explored key ideas with me and helped illuminate them. Ari Andricopoulos endlessly read and advised and edited drafts and told me what to cross out. Chloe Andricopoulos, Naomi Jaffe, Clare Manifold, Manya McClew, Julie McNamara, Altazar Rossiter, Robin Shohet, Raj Thamotheram, Bridget Towers, Myron Walters, Geoff Warburton and Jurgen Woolf have all devoted time and energy to reading drafts of the book and helping me make it what it is now. All my friends and family supported and encouraged me throughout. Thank you all.

The many 'burnout people'[1] – whose insights and stories are at the heart of this book have been my inspiration. The honesty, intelligence, courage and humour with which they were able to understand and find their way through burnout and beyond helped me to see what was really important. Their willingness to open their hearts and reveal their soul whisperings was profoundly moving. I have a special debt of thanks to Sue Townsend who so generously offered not only her time but the use of her own name in talking openly and therefore publicly of deep and private areas of her life.

My wonderful editor Rowena Webb at Hodder and Stoughton, by valuing this book from the beginning, helped me to believe in it, and by reading early drafts, pointed the way to make it a better book. Emma Heyworth-Dunn and the whole team at Hodder are a remarkable, warm and encouraging group of women who welcomed me and my book with open arms. My great agent, Andrew Lownie, helped turn an idea into a book. Thank you all.

On another level, I honour all the soul food that has made this book possible – my inner soul community, the world of images and the books that light my way.

As always, the mistakes are mine. Whatever is good is the gift of my inner and outer community. May you, the reader, gain pleasure and sustenance from this gift.

Contents

1

The Hidden Message of Burnout
Introducing the Joy of Burnout

Burnout feels like the end of the world. It's not. It's the beginning of a new one. I know because burnout turned my life around. At the time, I didn't even know what it was called. Once I understood what had happened to me, a lot of things fell into place.

A few autumns ago, I was sitting in a café with my friend Ilene who had made a surprise trip from Sweden to be with me on my birthday. We chatted about work and she mentioned that in Sweden, burnout was hitting the headlines as one of the biggest problems of the country's industry.

I heard the word 'burnout' as if for the first time, and a light went on in my brain: *Burnout – that's it!*

Until that moment, I hadn't seen the 'stress breakdown' I'd suffered ten years before as burnout. When the worst of it was over, a consultant told me I'd had ME or chronic fatigue. While it was happening, my NHS doctor said, 'You need a holiday . . . not on the National Health, I'm afraid.' A homeopathic doctor told me, 'My dear, your heart is tired.'

Burnout just hadn't been on my radar screen.

Yet the word 'burnout' was so powerful that it propelled me on the search that led to this book. It seems to have this evocative power not just for me but for many other people as well. I sat at a party and mentioned that I was researching burnout. Eyes lit up all around me. Everyone sitting near me had a story. I asked participants on one of our Thailand holidays, 'How many of you have burnt out or are burning out?' Eighty per cent of hands went up. I inquired of friends and colleagues, 'Do you know anyone who has burnt out?' Almost invariably they replied, 'Yes, me, and loads of other people I know.'

Often, like me, they hadn't thought of what had happened to them as burnout, but when they heard the word, they knew it had something to say to them. Indeed, the term 'burnout' seemed to spread like wildfire (pun unintended) as soon as the concept was introduced in the 1970s. The word was used internationally, often without being translated from English. It even appears on jazzy designer T-shirts.

I am not sure why burnout has such resonance. The word speaks, I think, to the part of us that wants to burn on with the fire of life, love, passion, challenge and meaning and it describes our devastation when that fire seems to have burnt itself out. It vividly captures, also, the nature of the experience. People who have burnt out describe it in terms such as 'I could almost feel my brain burning' or 'It was like my nervous system was fried' or 'Instead of growing like a tree, I was a pile of ash.'

For me, it also has another subliminal meaning. It reminds me that the phoenix rises from ashes, and that burnout is really a message of renewal.

When we burn out, it is our old personality that burns itself out. Then our soul fire begins to light our way and to bring us joy.

This book tells the story of burnout, of why and how we burn out, and what we can do about it. But the 'what we can do about it' is paradoxical, because above all what we need to do is stop doing and start listening to ourselves in a completely new way.

What is burnout?

Burnout is one of the words that seem to define this moment in history. No longer an unusual event, it has become part of a normal life cycle, along with midlife crisis, stress, and serious chronic illness, all of which have connections with burnout. And rather than being a one-off event, it can recur again and again in different forms as we grapple with certain fundamental issues. It often begins in a single sphere of our lives, but it can tend to spread everywhere.

The classic signs of burnout are:

- A growing emotional, mental and/or physical exhaustion which isn't alleviated by sleeping
- An increasing sense of being cut off from ourselves and other people
- A decreasing ability to be effective at doing what we have always done, either at work or at home.

Of these, exhaustion is the most defining characteristic. Each of us has our own individual pattern of burnout, and there is a range of symptoms that can alert us to the fact that we have begun to burn out. These include:

- Extreme tiredness; inability to relax or have a restful sleep; emotional deadness; chronic anger; high self-criticism; loss of appetite for food, sex, life; feelings of being trapped, distant, disillusioned, cynical, hollow, pleasureless and humourless
- Poor attention; speeding up without increased effectiveness
- An increase in watching TV, drinking alcohol, eating junk food, shopping, playing computer games, using Internet chat rooms, pursuing casual sex or seeking any form of escape that is addictive
- A closing down from family, friends, colleagues, bosses and/or clients
- An increase in physical problems ranging from back problems, heart pains, head pains, frozen shoulder or loss of libido to chronic fatigue/ME, adrenal and thyroid problems, irritable bowel syndrome, post-viral illnesses, viral meningitis and even heart attacks.

We are tired, we are angry, we can't relax, we are often in physical pain, there seems little point to anything we are doing, and we don't like ourselves or anyone else very much. Indeed, we hardly recognize ourselves as the people we used to be. Yet those of us headed for serious burnout just battle on and on. We over-ride all our danger signals and work harder and harder until one day we stop and listen and take action, or we become so incapacitated that we have no choice but to stop.

If we are forced finally to stop work or other activities for what we tell ourselves will be a few days, even though we may never have taken more than a day or two of sick leave in our lives, we sometimes find the time stretching into weeks, months, even into a decision to resign. We may be seriously ill, emotionally empty, exhausted beyond belief.

Gemma, psychotherapist, aged thirty-nine when she burnt out, described this exhaustion:

> *It was all I could do to lie in bed and stare at the ceiling. Anything more than a white wall was exhausting. I could feel physically ill if I looked at colour. I was so exhausted I felt like my body would stop breathing because there wasn't the energy to breathe. I wondered if this was what it is like to be old.*

We are bound to think we have done something wrong, or that something is wrong with us, or that the world has treated us badly. And yet, if we did but know it, burnout is so powerfully transformative that it appears to be a signal not of failure, but of a challenge to create a new way of life. In fact burnout is probably the best thing that ever happened to us.

Carl's story

To give you a real-life picture of how burnout can work, I'd like to tell you Carl's story. Carl was a high-flying manager of a medium-sized company who burnt out when he was in his early forties. He is typical in many ways of the many people I have known who have gone through burnout. He is bright, ambitious, likable and a high achiever. He loved his work and was immensely energetic. He rose quickly into top management, ate up challenges and never believed he had limits.

Carl had a broad vision of how Information Technology could transform the business he worked for and was delighted when he was appointed director of IT. The project soon grew too big for him to handle alone but he didn't request additional staff. Not long after-

4

wards, a small board of directors was formed. He wasn't invited to join it, whilst two of his close colleagues were.

Thus at a time when he was giving more than his all, Carl felt undermined and undervalued by his boss and was shut out of the circle of his peers. He didn't challenge his boss's decision because he was so upset and humiliated, nor could he overcome the combination of independence, pride and need for approval that stopped him from asking for help with his project. He just denied that any of it was important, pushed down his feelings and did what he always did: worked harder and harder.

Before long he was experiencing chest pains and mild depression and found himself sighing without knowing why. His judgment became clouded and he began to suffer from insomnia. He was angry and impatient a lot of the time and distracted himself with television and fantasies about the future. His marriage suffered as he stopped confiding in anyone, including his wife. He drove himself even harder until he developed a flu which turned into post-viral syndrome and kept him off work for months.

When he finally returned to work, he was appointed to the board and, as part of a reorganization, became second in command, working closely with his boss, coaching him and creating a new vision. His energy was high and he was firing on all cylinders.

But when his boss stopped relying on Carl and even got in someone new to coach him, the stress feelings returned along with the driven work, emotional shutdown and illness. Carl became so ill with ME/chronic fatigue that he resigned from his job, and soon afterwards, his wife 'resigned' from their marriage.

Having lost the shape of his life as he knew it, Carl faced despair. But before long he discovered the wonders of having space in his life. He regained his usual determination and optimism, but this time directed his energy towards getting healthy, finding out who he really was, working towards a sense of community and revisioning his life.

Now, five years later, he has a new life: a new career as a successful coach of business leaders, a new relationship in which he strives to stay open and intimate, and a new sense of himself. As he puts it, '*Burnout was life catching up with me, creating the space for the real me to emerge.*'

You are not alone

I would not be writing this book if I had not burnt out and found it such a remarkable opportunity for a more joyful life that I have always been thankful for it, despite the costs. The story of what happened to me is told at the end of this chapter, complete with a surprising twist of fate.

Nor would I be writing this book if my life hadn't always involved a commitment to working with myself and others to find and express our truth and joy. I have been a psychotherapist, a group leader, a consultant and a senior lecturer in psychology and social psychology. I have run training workshops around the world in Imagework, my self-help approach to tapping into the inner images that guide our lives, which is the subject of my book *Life Choices, Life Changes*.[1] Since 1979 I have, with my former husband, founded and directed two holistic holiday centres on the Greek island of Skyros, as well as winter centres first in Tobago and then in Thailand. This lifelong direction is what inspires this book.

Through my people-work background, I have had the privilege of working with, talking deeply to, or corresponding with about seventy-five men and women who have burnt out. Together we explored what it all meant and where it was leading them. I include here clients, students, course participants, friends, colleagues and members of various relevant networks.

Their occupations when they burnt out include: airline planner, artist, banking lawyer, chemist, consultant, engineer, geophysicist, headhunter, health practitioner, insurance broker, journalist, manager, managing director, overseas development worker, psychotherapist, singer, social worker, teacher and writer. Their ages at the time of burnout ranged between late twenties and mid fifties. Several of them burnt out more than once.

Reading the extensive research literature was invaluable to me, but it was these in-depth explorations and sharings that enabled me to get a profound and subtle understanding of the inner experience of burnout. Several of the 'people of burnout' I talked to or worked with have kindly permitted me to quote them here, either giving their real first names or using a change of name. One, the writer Sue

Townsend, tells her story under her own name as her identity is so intrinsic to her experience.

All my people-work activities gave me a wonderfully creative life doing work I loved. But, along with raising small children, they also added up to a life as overfull and driven as those of most of the 'burnout people' I have known. Yet working too hard and being overstressed for years did not burn me out.

I started on the burnout trail only when I was ready to make a different choice, and went back to my old ways instead. Burnout was a sign that I had no option but to listen to myself even better and follow where my real self was asking me to go. This is what I have done, and I would like to support you to do so too, if it seems right to you. It is the path of Radical Healing.

This book is my way of bringing you the insights that have helped me and others through and beyond burnout. I want to reach out to those of you who are, or have been, in similar situations and say: *You are not alone, it is not wrong or bad for you to be where you are, and there is a way forward. It is the way to joy.*

Is burnout new?

Let us backtrack for a moment to look at the history of burnout. In the sixteenth century, St John of the Cross wrote *The Dark Night of the Soul*[2] about the experience of mystics who, after an experience of God's grace, went through despair, aridity and loss of connection with God. This phase was seen as a necessary one in the soul's journey towards purification. The 'dark night of the soul' could be considered a religious forerunner of what is now called burnout, and is a phrase that people who are burning out often use about themselves.

In literature, too, burnout was described long before the concept was identified by social scientists. In his great novel *Buddenbrooks*,[3] written at the turn of the twentieth century, Thomas Mann comprehensively depicted the process of burnout through his character Consul Thomas Buddenbrook.

More recently, the word 'burnout' itself has been used in a variety of different contexts. It is applied to drug takers who get to the end of the road and become like walking zombies. Among lawyers who work in poor communities, it refers to those who start off full of fire and enthusiasm and end up disillusioned and deadened. In sports it describes the effect of having overtrained. Graham Greene used the term 'burnt-out case'[4] in his novel of that title for lepers who came for treatment too late and had to wait until the disease burnt itself out, taking whatever limbs it was going to take. His main character, Querry, an architect who had lost his faith and his ability to love, also considered himself a 'burnt-out case'.

It wasn't until the late 1970s and early 1980s that social scientists began to pick up the word 'burnout' and use it in relation to work. Herbert Freudenberger,[5] who is given credit for using the word first, and Christina Maslach,[6] who defined it and applied a research perspective, were the pioneers. Burnout immediately caught the imagination of people all over the world. When I began my library research, I found over 7,000 entries for burnout on one database. In general, the research is about work burnout. There has been a little study of marriage burnout, but mainly this is about burnt-out relationships,[7] rather than about people who have actually burnt out as a result of a relationship, a subject which is covered in this book.

Originally, burnout was widely thought of as an individual clinical problem and has been attributed to a variety of causes: failure to retain one's idealized self-image, lack of balance in one's life, progressive disillusionment, wrong expectations, poor coping mechanisms when goals are frustrated, a failed quest for existential meaning, a lack of social competence, or extreme emotional overload.

Burnout was then shown to be far more prevalent in some professions or organizations than in others. It began to be seen as an organizational problem resulting from: a high level of demands and responsibility; a low level of support and appreciation; a lack of control or decision-making power; a dearth of resources to carry out the job; and the loss of meaning and community. At first it was associated with social workers, nurses and workers in the caring professions, the people carrying all the responsibility and the emotional demands but holding very little decision-making power. Soon it became clear that this was happening throughout industry as well.

Some researchers and clinicians argue that since some people burn out in the best situations and others never burn out, no matter what happens, burnout is best described as the result of a lack of fit between the individual and his work situation. Other researchers have considered burnout to be the symptom of a materialistic and alienating society.

Burnout is considered to be increasing rapidly and dangerously. Estimates of its incidence have ranged between 10 per cent and 80 per cent of the working population. In Japan, *karoshi*, 'death by overwork', which is often associated with burnout, is becoming a major social concern. Burnout is commonly described as having reached epidemic or even pandemic proportions.[8]

An incomplete picture

The research on burnout is wide-ranging and fascinating, and the threads of what I believe burnout is about are all there in the literature. But what hasn't emerged is a complete picture. This is because the literature is focused too narrowly on work situations, and, more importantly, because burnout is seen as a problem or illness that needs to be fixed or cured or prevented.

I am in the rather unusual position of arguing that although there is a great deal wrong with our society, our work-places, our relationships and our lives, burnout is ultimately positive if we are open to its message. This is because it asks us to become more who we really are. Indeed, it is part of an evolutionary process that is happening at all levels of our personal and social lives.

The word 'epidemic', like many of the words associated with burnout, makes it sound as if something terrible is happening. Epidemics must be stopped so that life as we knew it before can go on. But life as we knew it before cannot go on. We are being pushed by burnout towards that which we do not yet know but are yearning to discover. This is why the prevalence of burnout is in many ways a good though painful omen.

The message of burnout

Burnout is not just something that happens to people when they work too hard or have too much stress or don't like their jobs. It is not the direct result of inhumane, unfair or overdemanding situations at work. All of these contribute to burnout but don't cause it. It is not the same as mid-life crisis, but mid-life crises can be forms of burnout. It is not depression, though depression can be involved. It is not related only to work, though it does have to do with how we use our creativity. Nor is burnout a modern epidemic that needs to be arrested.

The message of this book is that burnout is the state of mind, body and spirit reached by those of us who have come to the end of a particular road but haven't acknowledged this.

Burnout announces this fact in the strongest possible terms. It can emerge out of any situation or relationship where we put our creativity at the service of our passion, our heart, our belief, our identity or our belonging. And rather than being cured, burnout needs to be honoured and listened to.

Burnout is, or rather can be, a door to walk through into a life with space, love and joy – indeed, a sense of being able to be one's true self.

In fact, burning out is a sign that we have already begun to know something about our true self that we are not quite ready to tell ourselves. Some voice of truth inside whispers to us that our old ways of relating are not working and we need to stop, rethink and find a new way forward. We don't dare to. Yet we cannot afford not to.

We are evolving beings, becoming more and more conscious of the true direction of our lives. The more we evolve, the greater the cost to us of not following our intuitive longings. It can be literally fatal for us not to do what on some level we know we are meant to do.

Burnout is the result of having become better able to hear our soul but not yet daring to listen. Burnout demands that we listen.

People who have been through burnout and listened to what it had to teach them feel grateful for the experience, even if they are still suffering from its effects. They know burnout stopped them from doing or being something they no longer wanted to do or be. Most are amazed that they could have lived that way, and some are equally amazed that they managed to get out of it.

Edward, an engineer at the time he burnt out, told me, *'If it weren't for my burnout I don't think I would be around today. It saved my life.'*

What does joy have to do with it?

Where does joy fit in? Joy, as I am referring to it in this book, has a rather specific meaning. It is not happiness or contentment or excitement. These relate to being satisfied or even thrilled with our present-life situation. Joy has nothing to do with our life situation. It has to do with the love of life itself.

Joy emerges in the spaces rather than in the content of our lives. It is what happens when, even for a moment, we feel totally free, with a sense of space around us and inside us. The colours become more vivid, and a laugh bubbles up naturally. Joy may be experienced alone or with others. It may occur when we connect to nature or to a child's smile. It may emerge after hours of meditation or just a momentary glimpse of the blue lining of a bird's wing. It may even happen when everything has gone wrong and we just start to laugh and laugh at the sheer surreal irony of it all.

At that moment, our life situation doesn't matter. Life itself is our joy. Being ourselves is our delight.

Burning out could almost be defined as joylessness. We have lost contact with the Divine Comedy, that ability to laugh compassionately at the terrible and wonderful ways in which life works itself out. Yet burnout forces us to take a step towards joy. We won't stop, so burnout stops us. We won't make a space for ourselves, so we burn out and all we have is space. And it is out of that space that the joy eventually comes.

Mary, airline planner, returned to the same job and same life situation after being burnt out but felt very different inside. She described her emerging joy.

It's just waking up in the morning thinking, 'Today is going to be good. There's so much to look forward to.' I'm not living in the future anymore, saying, 'It will be good when . . .' It's good now. I'm at peace with myself, not beating myself up about things. I know I'm quite a nice person, the sun's going to shine, and I'm going to talk to my best friends and we'll have a life.

You don't have to burn out to chart your new course

You don't have to go through the devastating effects of a full-blown forest-fire-type burnout to learn its lessons. My hope is that this book will help you change direction before you burn out completely. If it's too late for that, you will understand better why you burntout and what is good about it. Either way, you can learn to appreciate the message of burnout and take the path of Radical Healing to a new way of living.

In my experience, once we acknowledge the true meaning of our burnout – or of our first signs of burnout – we are able to let go of old unhelpful patterns of thought and action and begin to chart our course for a new way of life.

Individuals who are highly prone to burnout can be among the most creative, dynamic, loving, and focused people in our society. They have driven themselves all their lives, often in the service of others, and are now having to learn a new way to drive and a new direction to drive in.

If we cooperate with what burnout is teaching us, a vast creative potential can be redirected to benefit not only us, but also our loved ones, our organizations, and society as a whole.

How to read this book

The Joy of Burnout enables you to put your experience of burnout into a framework that is positive and understandable, and to find a new way forward to a life enhanced by joy. If you are concerned with burnout not for yourself but for people you care for or are responsible for, this book can help you understand them better and be of more service to them.

The chapters

Chapters 2 and 3 describe the social and personal forces that have made burnout so prevalent, the typical profile of people prone to burnout, and the burnout process itself, including a soul perspective on the meaning of burnout. There is a checklist to help you see if you are burning out. Chapters 4–9 describe the actual steps we take to move from wholeheartedness to burnout and why we take them. Chapters 10–15 outline the stages of Radical Healing from burnout to joy.

Along the way I use quotes and stories of the 'burnout people' I have worked with as well as my own experiences. There are also questions to ask yourself and exercises to try. As always, the more we put in, the more we gain. But don't be put off if exercises are just not your thing. Considering how all this applies to you may be your form of exercise.

Too exhausted or too busy to read?

You may be in that burning-out or burnt-out stage when reading a whole book feels exhausting. If so, begin by reading the introductory first section and the last two sections of each chapter (**Consider This** . . . or **Try This** . . . and **Finally** . . .), and, if possible, try out an exercise. Or you may just want to open the book to a page randomly and see where your eye falls. That can be enough on a day when your energy is really low.

On the other hand, if you think you might be burning out but you are *much* too busy to read a book about it, I would strongly advise the opposite strategy. Take a deep breath and commit yourself to read every word from start to finish and do the exercises religiously. You probably need this and more to stop you before it's too late.

Window-shopping

Above all, always refer back to your own intuition and your own experience. Read this book as if you were window-shopping – see what you like, go in and try it on, but don't buy anything that doesn't feel good or fit you really well.

Using your creative imagination

Many of the exercises in this book are based on using your imagination to gain a new perspective on your life and to find a positive way forward. These are a few principles to introduce you to the use of imagery:

- Imagery has been shown time and again to deepen and speed up any healing, learning or creative process, whether it be recovery from an illness or becoming a better football player or business manager or writer. Successful, highly skilled, healthy and creative people use imagery naturally.
- To work with our images, we do not need to be able to conjure up visual pictures. Images can be felt, heard, smelled, tasted or otherwise sensed as well as seen. Everyone can tap into their images, just as everyone can dream, and it gets easier and easier with practice.
- One of the advantages of images is that we can look at ourselves from different perspectives and gain the kind of objectivity we don't usually have about ourselves. We can also experience memories from the past or pictures of the future as if they are happening right now, getting the benefits of foresight and hindsight without ever leaving our chair.
- Whenever you are working with an image, take the time to get as many of your senses going as you can. See the colours, hear the sounds, feel the feelings. Look at the image or memory picture from the outside or from above. Then step into the picture and 'become' the person you were. Take time to imagine being that person, breathing as that person, sitting or standing as that person, until you feel you can see the world through their eyes.
- It would be good to have a notebook or file in which to record your experiences, insights, thoughts and feelings as you work your way through this book. You might also like to tape the instructions and then listen to them, or better still, work with a friend.

- You can find more information about using imagery in Chapter 9 and in my book, *Life Choices, Life Changes*.

Consider This: Is this book for you?

- Does the word burnout ring bells for you – or irritate you?
- Are you burning out or burnt out?
- Have you burnt out in the past and feel you don't fully understand what happened or how to prevent it from happening again?
- Do you know someone else – a colleague, a friend, a partner, a team member, a boss or even your doctor or dentist – who may be burning out?
- Are you willing to consider that burnout may be telling you something important about your life that goes beyond overwork or overstress?
- Do you feel there is something about the way you use your creative energy that doesn't work any more?
- Are you willing to begin to listen to yourself more deeply even if it may be painful at first?
- Does bringing more joy into your life feel important enough to do something about it?
- Are you wanting to encourage someone else who may be burning out to take some positive steps for themselves?

If the answer to any of these questions is 'Yes', why not read further?

Finally: Burnout – ugh!

Last week, when I phoned my friend Natalie, I told her I was writing a book on burnout. She just said 'Burnout – ugh!' I added that it is called *The Joy of Burnout*, and she said, 'Oooh, that makes me feel sick to my stomach. Burnout is so awful. What does it have to do with joy?'

Yet when I tell people who have been burnt out and have come through it about my odd book title, they invariably laugh and say, 'Great, go for it. It's so important.'

They know about the joy.

Transform or Die: My Burnout Story

It was October 1989. I was forty-four. I had just celebrated the publication of my first book and had also resigned from my full-time lecturing job of seventeen years. I felt I had done enough for one lifetime. It was time to rest.

I was feeling better than I had for a very long time. During the two or three years leading up to this period I had begun to confront one after another of the attitudes that were driving me towards overwork and overgiving, and to take my own needs and longings more seriously. One of the effects of my father's death during this period was to throw into sharp relief how much of a struggle my life had been. I had committed myself not to let that continue. The lectureship had been the first thing to go.

My kids were no longer babies, nor were the centres my husband and I had created. I had gained enough financial security to make it possible to have a lighter work schedule. I was still seeing clients, running courses, co-organizing and running our Skyros holidays, and co-parenting our children. But by comparison with what I had been doing before, I could look forward to an easier life.

I knew that to find a new way forward, I would need to let go of even more of my activities and go within. I longed to do this but I felt frightened. One afternoon during the summer before these events, I sat with my old friend and colleague, Max, in a taverna by the sea on the island of Skyros and told him of my hopes and fears. I started to cry. Didn't I need to be out there, visible to all, doing and giving, for me to have any love at all? Who would follow me into my retreat and love me?

Max looked at me lovingly and talked to me of how he had more than once gone on his own retreat, and people had come and knocked on his door. He had not been forgotten. Then he said something which I didn't fully understand at the time but which rang in my ears years later: 'There is a word in Sanskrit for what happens when a householder has come to the time in his life when he must turn over the keys of the household to his children and go on his path but instead, he continues with his old life.'

I've forgotten the word in Sanskrit, but I suspect that the word in

English is 'burnout'. Less than two months later, I didn't go on my own path and I burnt out.

Just this one last time

I have noticed that at the moment when we are almost ready to follow a new direction, it often happens that something comes up that is dripping with everything we are addicted to and we say, 'Just this one last time.'

In my case, I was asked to engage in an enormous project – a new magazine. It would demand all my energy, commit me to a crippling mortgage – which meant I would lose the financial security I was depending on – and open up my house to a staff of people who would leave me not a single room to call my own. Moreover, it would not be my own project – I would just be assisting without having any decision-making power.

What a crazy thing to do. Of course I said no.

I didn't. I said yes. The person that asked me to do it was my husband, the project seemed a good one, and despite all my commitments to myself, I still had more of a need to please him and make him happy, especially for a 'good cause', than I had to listen to my own inner voice.

Having come to a point in my life when I was more in touch with myself and also less ruled by necessity, I was more able to hear my soul and was in a better position to listen and follow. But I was not free enough from my old needs and fears to do so.

Burning out

So there I was, with people in my sitting room, people in the entrance hall, people in my study and people in my kitchen, all sitting in front of computers with telephones by their sides. There also happened to be decorators in my bedroom, repairing the effect of subsidence. The only place I could be alone was the bathroom, and even that had two doors, only one of which locked.

The summer before I'd had repetitive dreams about people in my house, culminating with one in which people were selling things in my front room. I now had people selling advertising in my front room.

In order to do what we know is not right for us, it is necessary to cut ourselves off from our own inner messages. I was upset about what was going on in my home, and felt that no one was listening to my needs. But as I discounted these myself, I hardly noticed.

There wasn't any more pressure on me than there had been before; in fact, the reverse was true. But all those years, I thought I had no choice but to do what I was doing. Now I knew I did have a choice. Then I was wholehearted. Now, having seen another way, I was divided against myself, though I didn't consciously admit this.

I thought I could handle it. At least I kept up my swimming, which was the symbol of my new self-care. But each time I left the house, staff members sitting in the hall would say in a friendly way, 'Where are you going?' and I'd feel embarrassed. After all they were working, so why wasn't I?

It got worse. The work piled up and money was being spent at a vast and frightening rate. I starting speeding around faster and faster like a wound-up toy, trying to attend to everything at once, though I was not ultimately the one in control. And because my husband and I weren't getting on, he was angry with me but still expecting my devotion to the cause. I worked even harder to try to gain back his approval.

I glanced at the television and wondered why the characters were moving so slowly. 'Why don't they get on with it?' I wondered.

It might have looked as if this high speed and high stress were burning me out; in fact these were the result rather than the cause of the burnout process. I was doing that very common thing of going faster and faster down a path I knew I shouldn't have been on at all.

I went for a medical checkup related to the mortgage we were taking out. The doctor looked at me and said, 'Your blood pressure is rather high.' During the last medical checkup I'd had, only a few weeks before, the doctor thought I was glowing with good health. I was surprised at this deterioration in my health but had no time to worry about it.

One day I walked out of the house and simply couldn't go home. I stood in the middle of central London's Piccadilly not knowing what to do. The noises sounded too loud to bear and my head hurt badly. I took refuge in a cinema which was showing the new film *Shirley*

Valentine and I watched Shirley finding a new life for herself against all odds.

I came home after the end of the working day when all the staff had gone, my head pounding as if there were men tunnelling in my brain. The pain was horrific. The next day, I had absolutely no energy. I felt like a car which was operating on one cylinder. Whenever I tried to make a phone call, write a letter or make a decision, my brain simply ground to a halt. It was a No Go area.

The ghost in the attic

It transpired that this was the start of a long-term health and energy breakdown, and that these symptoms were to continue for many years. The things I now found impossible to do were those I had never enjoyed – the administration, the decisions, the endless letters and phone calls, all of which had increased exponentially with this new project. For years after I burnt out, neither my aching brain nor my exhausted body would let me do this work: they seemed simply to go on strike. This work ate up energy I didn't have.

Yet, in a limited way, and by taking lots of breaks, even at my most burnt-out I could still do therapy and run my training courses, and even managed to direct sessions in Greece. This was the work I had always loved; it was my soul work and it nourished me.

In my groups, when we took turns at finding images of our lives, a typical one for me was: 'I am a ghost in the attic.' When there was a break, or at the end of the working week, I'd stay in my room, close the shutters or pull the curtains, and just close down. Even light felt like a demand.

After I recovered significantly from the worst aspects of this, I could still only be active for two-thirds of a normal day. I had to rest in bed either all afternoon or all evening. But neither my colleagues nor my students and clients guessed how bad I was feeling. I appeared okay in public, and just hid when my energy fell way below zero and I was desperate.

I did let my friends see what was going on. As a result, for the first time I began to develop what I had always wanted during those driven years, a group of friends who really loved and cared for me – and who would come out to play. Apparently, they needed to see that I was vulnerable before they could fully open their hearts to me. Or maybe I needed to see this before I could open my own heart. Anyway, I now had time to walk in the park with my friends because I couldn't do much else.

What do you do?

It was more than seven years before I had my full energy back. Even so, I have suffered relapses more than once, and old symptoms still trouble me when I put the wrong kind of pressure on myself. In fact, it is hard to say whether I ever got my full energy back in the sense of being able to live the life I used to live – because I no longer want to live the life I used to live. It seems impossible even to conceive of doing so.

During the years since my original moment of burnout, I have made wide-reaching changes in my life. The fruits of what I learnt are in this book. In the process, I have let go of most of my old work, commitments and identities and have suffered more than one 'dark night of the soul'. I no longer know what to answer when people ask, 'What do you do?' I can only say what I am doing right now or what I used to do. Yet once I had so many answers.

What did I gain in return? The following come to mind:

- A treasuring of being with myself and an honouring of my own rhythms.
- A tribe of people around the world who hold me in a loving and laughing web.
- A head that is often empty of thoughts and worries.
- So much less fear and self-attack and need to please or to be needed.
- A new way to create and contribute.
- A freedom from needing to know what is coming next.
- A feeling that no matter what is coming next I will be okay.
- A sense of my soul path, and a commitment to put this first.
- A feeling that in and around me there is great joy.

On reflection, I could summarize by saying: I have more or less got myself back after having given myself away all my life. Now I am free to surrender.

I have not found an end to struggle pain, doubt, unhappiness, anxiety or old patterns, nor do I expect I ever will. I have less of these, and I can usually take a loving perspective on them. But my childhood dreams of living happily ever after have definitely been dashed.

Yet I now understand the meaning of joy. And when it seems to vanish, I can ask myself, *Where is my joy now?* and have some idea how and where to find it.

My second life

Even at the time I became so ill, I was very grateful for being stopped. I was convinced that if I hadn't been, a heart attack or a stroke might have stopped me, perhaps for good. I had this image of having been in a speeding car and throwing myself out before it crashed. I had got hurt, but not killed.

And here a curious and rather stunning fact emerges to enlighten us about the meaning of this breakdown. Twenty-five years before these events, when I was in college, one of my professors had asked us to write our own obituaries as an exercise in the creative imagination.

My obituary had turned out to be rather prophetic. In fact, by the time I burnt out, I had lived out or done most of the things in the obituary, though in a somewhat different form, including the book I had just published.

But it was not until many years after this breakdown that a friend asked me when, according to the obituary, I had died. I dug it out and looked it up. I 'died' in a car crash at the end of October 1989 at the age of forty-four. This was exactly when these burnout events occurred.

It seems that somewhere in the programming of my being I had a choice: die or transform. Death and transformation stalked each other at that moment, and by having a death within life, transformation won out.

I was given a second life. It was my chance to find my joy.

The Burnout Trail:
From Wholeheartedness to Burnout

2

Don't Take It Too Personally
Burnout: The Bigger Picture

When I went through all those years of illness and exhaustion following my burnout, I felt as if I was the only one in the world having this experience. Later, as I spoke about what had happened to me, I began to hear a few stories that sounded like my own. Once I identified the experience as burnout, the trickle of stories became a deluge. Not only was I not alone, but for once in my life I was part of a trend!

As I analysed my own experience, read the research on burnout and talked deeply with people who have burnt out, a pattern began to emerge that made sense not only of the events in my own life, but of the rising importance of burnout in the technological societies of the developed world. This chapter discusses the nature of this pattern and what part we need to play in it to find a positive way forward.

In my view, the increase in burnout is a sign that something is changing for the better which has not yet gone for enough. Central to this positive change is the revolution in the role of choice and meaning in our lives.

More and more of us believe that we are able consciously to choose and create a meaningful life, and that we really want to do so. But this vision is not always matched by the realities of the work-place, our relationships or our lives. Furthermore, we haven't yet fully understood the nature of choice. The vision has gone ahead of a reality that can support it, both in the external world and in our own personal evolution. This is not surprising: it is how change and evolution work in a period of transition between old and new ways of being.

Because of the clash between our dreams and our present reality, there are many moments in which we are faced with conflict and disillusionment. One way or another, we are all being challenged to acknowledge our confusion, to locate our emerging truth and to live by it. If burnout is the form that this challenge to live truthfully takes in your life, then beginning to burn out is exactly the right incentive to help you take your next step towards joy.

Choosing a meaningful life

For large groups of people in Western technological societies, there has been a movement away from simple practical necessity and social certainty towards a proliferation of choice. In some ways, life with less choice protected us from burnout. Where necessity and certainty ruled, we knew what we had to do and the very fact that we *had* to do it was meaning enough. Our social structures and socially provided meanings held us as long as we played our roles and believed in them. Our connections with the community, with the earth, with the seasons, with ritual and with the everyday ordering of our lives supported us.

But necessity isn't what it used to be and neither is certainty. As we move towards having greater choice, our understanding of meaning changes. We need to find our own meanings and follow where they lead us, not just in the big decisions in life but from moment to moment. Even what is necessary needs to be ordered and prioritized in ever more complicated lists. It is not always obvious what to do and how to do it, or even which things are really necessary and which are not.

The privilege of choice and the challenge of uncertainty

As a woman, I feel particularly keenly that I have been privileged to belong to one of the first generations of women who believe that it is not exceptional to be in a financial, political, social and personal position to negotiate their own lives. This growing awareness of personal choice is also true in a somewhat different way for men.

As women change, men have had to respond if they were not to be dinosaurs. But more importantly for men, work situations are changing so that old roles do not hold them firmly in their place. This change affects both men and women, but for men it is far more disruptive of old assumptions.

Less than half the working population now have full-time permanent jobs: the rest are self-employed, on temporary contracts, part-timers or unemployed. More and more people are running their own businesses and charting their own course. Retirement is also seen as a creative period in which to engage in something new rather than simply withdraw from the old.

Management guru Charles Handy,[1] who has been predicting and charting this change for years, writes of how when he joined Shell at the age of twenty-one he was shown his pension plan which, he was reassured, would provide well for his future widow. Apparently, people didn't live more than an average of eighteen months after they retired from Shell. Now this way of funding the meaning of our lives is on its way out, along with some of those well-endowed pension funds.

As certainties are challenged, the world is no longer supplying the answers it once did. For many men and women, spiritual beliefs that guide people to look within have begun to take the place of institutional religions, while, in contrast, fundamentalism is rapidly increasing. International travel and media coverage expose us to unfamiliar cultures that can lead us to question our assumptions about our own culture. Politicians of all parties seem out of the reach of the general public, accessible mainly to big business and big media, and they are proving unable to provide answers to the social challenges we face. 'Growth' and 'progress', the fruits of globalization, seem to be increasingly damaging societies and environments. Yet there appears to be no powerful viable alternative behind which we can put our energy and conviction.

As we are no longer able to find certainty in our social and political and religious worlds, we are forced to look within for answers. Life is demanding that we find our own way to understand what is happening and what to do about it.

This is in many ways extraordinarily hopeful, particularly as we find new ways to understand and choose. We are beginning to be guided not just by our heads but by our hearts and our souls and to exercise parts of ourselves we didn't think we needed, or didn't even know about. All this helps us to develop our full humanity. But in the process of learning how to do this, we will often fall into illusion and disillusionment.

The illusions of choice

In making the choices which shape our lives day by day and hour by hour, it is easy to develop false beliefs about the nature of choice. A common illusion is that if we can choose, we should be able to do it perfectly and, indeed, get everything we want. As we drive ourselves relentlessly to attain that happy, successful life, we can inadvertently eliminate any joy we once had. And if life is not perfect or we are not happy, it proves either that we have done something wrong or that someone has wronged us.

Our new understanding of the holistic nature of life, the fact that everything is interconnected, can be used to stress ourselves even further. We expect success to be demonstrated not only by our cars, our houses and our jobs but also by our level of emotional and spiritual development. One study of stress reduction courses in business showed that many participants actually increased their stress levels by adding yoga and meditation to all their other 'shoulds'.[2]

A large menu can appear to give a choice, but what happens if all the dishes are made up of roughly the same ingredients which are neither tasty nor healthy? Not every choice is a real choice. Many of the choices we are offered, ranging from drink, drugs, food, shopping, television and video games to all-consuming jobs, are actually a range of different ways to dull our relationship to our lives. They can help us cover up our feelings about being unable to find our way to the life we believe we should have.

Our background ideals and beliefs about choice serve a positive function when they inspire us to stretch our limits. But they also torture us with our failure to make the grade. When all is going well, we feel excited about the freedom to choose a meaningful life. When we are faced with contradictions that we cannot see our way through, making choices can become a stress and a threat to our self-esteem and our sense of integrity.

All is not going well

And all is not going well. While this revolution of higher expectations is happening in our individual and collective consciousness, there is in many ways a worsening of the social context at work and at home. Neither big business nor the 'big relationship' of marriage or committed sexual partnership is meeting our growing need for a meaningful investment of our creativity and love. Similarly, technology, having promised a life without limits, has driven us into stress, endangered our sense of community and led to a shorter and shorter attention span.

The confusion and disillusionment that result can make us very prone to burnout. As Professor Bruce Lloyd put it, 'Burnout happens when your life has lost meaning within the structures that you have committed yourself to.'[3] This loss of meaning has become an almost inevitable part of our lives.

Confusion in the work-place

When I was coming of age in the 1960s, things seemed clearer. We thought we could make an unambiguous choice between being 'in', in the sense of being part of the establishment with all its horrors and compromises and rewards, and dropping 'out', in the sense of holding on to our ideals. Since then, reality has become far more confusing.

Big businesses now speak the language of our idealism. They began by sending people to encounter groups, and slowly the 'welfare' of the staff, and the need for 'visions', the importance of 'personal development', and even access to therapy or 'coaching' as part of work training have become part of the ethos. Soul or spirit in business is now a hot topic.

Yet along with this come the downsizing, outsourcing, short-term contracts, erosion of unions and all the methods by which business has become leaner and meaner. Work loads are heavier, support networks cut, and the growing needs of employees to have a say and be treated fairly and in line with their values are often not respected. People working in the business world sometimes need those therapy sessions because they are being driven crazy by their work situations.

Alongside these contradictions in the world of business, the soft world of health, education and welfare has become tougher and tougher. The ivory towers and havens of social justice some of us thought we'd signed up for have become businesses, just poorer paid than the private sector. Frequently they are modelled after outdated business concepts and have a very mixed responsiveness to the increased power and expectations of clients or consumers.

The memory of the reorganization of one of the colleges I taught in comes to mind. We had a college 'typing pool', which consisted of a group of women working together in an office with a genuinely communal atmosphere, filled with humour and smiles for each other and for us lecturers. They always tried to meet our unreasonable requests for rush jobs on our reading lists and handouts. We were never made to feel a nuisance.

Then came the call to turn the college into something more like a business. It was reorganized in the general direction of having more and more administrators and less and less support staff. Instead of having one Director and his secretary, there was now a corridor full of Assistant Directors who 'needed' their own secretaries. The typing pool was dismembered, each of the typists hived off to another Assistant Director's office. The loss of that community felt like a death to all of us.

Burnout in people-work fields is often thought of as the result of our inability to cope with unlimited demands from clients, emotional overload and insufficient resources. While this is part of the truth, burnout is at least as likely to be related to the patterns of authority and relationships in the management and administration of these organizations. Linda, who worked in the field of HIV and AIDS, told me this story of the events that led up to her burnout.

I started having less and less faith in the direction the senior management was taking the organization, but they didn't want to hear anything that differed from their own view. I felt like I had the responsibility of being on the team without any possibility of having any input.

I was being asked almost daily to apply to be the Director of Client Services. I finally agreed. But after a three-hour screening by the search firm they employed, I was told that they had screened me out and were not going to interview me, but wanted me to help interview the other candidates. I was crushed (and confused).

Some months later, without talking to me about it first, they appointed me to the post and announced this change to the whole staff. I felt I had become a chess piece that they were moving around without paying any attention to what I needed or wanted. Still, I committed to doing what I could to make it work.

What was, for me, the final blow came when a very devoted staff person was suddenly fired, on the spot, for what seemed to me a relatively small mistake, and they did it in a horrible way, continually trashing her behind closed doors. That was when I hit what I consider complete burnout.

It was always clear to me that I did not lose faith in the work. I lost faith in the work relationships. And in my ability to make any difference in them.

✗ Those of us who left work in the public or voluntary sector often did so to become self-employed or start our own small businesses, just as those leaving full-time employment in big business did. Now, whether we are idealistic or not, we are all in business or in organizations run as businesses.

The amalgamation of a non-commercial idealism with new business realities can be seen in many other fields. The writer Margaret Drabble[4] recently gave what was to be her last public lecture, and spoke of the way writers are now pressurized to sell their own books through book tours, lectures, radio, television and every possible medium. They are no longer able to live a 'writerly life' because they are now performers in the literary circus. Writer Sue Townsend's story which follows at the end of this chapter is marked by her continual attempts to protect her art from being compromised by the commercial world.

And in the background, sometimes deep in our unconscious and sometimes right on the surface, we hold the awareness that no matter how much we personally succeed, there is an increasing distance between the haves and the have-nots. We may suffer the pain of the privileged if we succeed, and if we don't, we may suffer the pain of thinking that with all our advantages we are still not okay. Damned if we do and damned if we don't, and no clear direction forward.

The fragility of relationships of choice

For those of us trying to have good intimate relationships, there are also growing contradictions. Our choice has enlarged, our knowledge and skills have increased, but clarity eludes us more and more.

A central feature in the generational shift in relationships is the knowledge that it is possible to communicate effectively about what is going right and wrong in our relationships. As I write this, I can't help thinking of my mother who was in many ways an unusually forward-thinking woman, although she was born to a very traditional family in what was then Palestine. She did not play the normal feminine roles, and worked in two jobs as a Hebrew teacher until she died. Yet at home, she was caught by traditions she couldn't break. These expressed themselves most powerfully in what could not be spoken of.

She and my father lost a daughter at about the age of two, before I was born, and my mother aged dramatically after that, as her photos show. Yet, she never spoke of it and I didn't know of my sister's life and death until I asked an innocent question when I was about twelve. When I wondered why she had never told me, she said, 'I thought you don't talk of painful things.' There were also other family secrets that were too painful to talk of and yet shadowed the atmosphere of our lives.

I doubt that my mother and father ever truly communicated on a deep level about what was going wrong for both of them. The two subsisted rather than lived together, and became progressively more alienated from each other after we children left home.

At an age when she could have transformed her marriage or left to start a new life, my mother became ill with a heart condition and died. She was not much older than I am now, though I'm not sure of her exact age because this was another secret and passports were unreliable. We cannot of course say for sure why someone gets ill. But my feeling is that she had a choice: communicate or die. Even to separate, my parents would have had to communicate. I don't think my mother knew she had that choice. She would be very happy to know that I and my generation do.

Many of us in this generation have started reaching out for new definitions and new ways to love each other. Yet the old world still holds its own, not only out there but inside us. We are locked into old gender and relationship patterns from which it is hard to free ourselves, and so are the men and women we meet.

In the heterosexual world, which is the one I know best, understanding the differences between men and women is increasingly being seen as a key to successful relationships. Yes, we are indeed different and it may help us to understand each other better. But what about our ideals of how things could change? Can we transcend these differences or do we have to go back to old patterns?

And although we may have more awareness and choice than my mother did, we have a lot less commitment. We believe in the possibility of intimate relationships in which we can express our true selves, and we are willing to devote tremendous energy to working these out. Yet the reality is that we don't always manage to get past the first date or the first fight or the first intimacy. If we marry, we now have a one-in-three chance of divorcing, and the percentage is rising rapidly.[5] If we don't marry, the chances of separation are far higher. My friends in same-sex relationships tell me a similar story.

Relationships of choice are a new and fragile thing. Yet there is often a deep pain in being without a partner in a society without a sense of community to support us, and an equal pain in being with a partner if we can't be fully ourselves. The way forward eludes many of us.

Transition pain

So there we are, all dressed up but nowhere to go. We believe more and more in our ability and our right to make positive and meaningful choices, but the outer and inner realities do not make it easy to do that.

Often, there is no one to help us deal with this confusion and no time to think about it. The pressure on us to keep producing the goods we have always produced comes from inside us and from the outside world. We don't believe we will be of any use at all if we do not. We just put our trust in our work and relationships and become burnt out, disillusioned, angry and self-blaming.

Yet burnout is not our fault or someone else's, but rather exposes a fault-line that is there in all of us and in our society.

On one level, this fault-line is to do with the gap between ideals and reality. On another level, we can choose to see it more hopefully as being to do with the transition between that which is passing away and that which is coming to be. We have had a vision of how things could be. But the reality of how to make this true in the world always lags far behind. This is the nature of change.

Much of what we call reality consists of the structures based on old motivations that are still operating powerfully in our lives. Much of what we call the dream is based on yearnings towards that which may become reality in the future, once new structures have been created.

In a crisis, old and new visions and realities can collide. We are faced with situations we don't know how to negotiate, which challenge either our hopes and dreams or our old beliefs and habits and therefore require us to go out on a new edge. We can no longer operate within the framework of the work or relationship we are in. This can be very frightening.

What do we do in a crisis?

When our pictures don't fit reality, what do we do? Do we take refuge in certainty and choose a new orthodoxy which, as in the case of fundamentalism or nationalism or other dogmas, can set us against each other? Do we use the cultural means of escape, ranging from television to alcohol to sex to drugs? Do we find a new job or relationship and start all over again? Do we get angry and disillusioned and give up? Do we push down all our feelings and just work harder until we burn out?

Or do we step back, look at the realities, find our truth and move forward?

Linda told me how, at the poignant historical moment when it became clear that the HIV and AIDS epidemic couldn't be ended, others burnt out but she was able to step back and revision.

We deeply believed that if enough people knew what was going on, and knew how to take care of themselves and of others, the whole thing could turn around. We also believed that the government had the capability of stopping the whole thing if they would act quickly.

I hit a point of feeling like I was 'shovelling shit to the wind'. That no matter what we did, more and more people were getting infected and we couldn't stem the tide. That was the burnout point for many people who worked there.

But for me, it was only a pause, an adjustment of purpose. It was probably the point at which I realized that we weren't going to end the thing with love. But it became clear pretty quickly that we still made a huge difference by continuing to spend time one-on-one with clients.

When we do find a new way forward relying on our own truth, we are meeting the challenge set us by this moment in history. Yet we are not always able to do this. Linda herself burnt out when she could not deal with what went wrong in her relationship with her managers.

When the reality outside doesn't match what we expect, it often hits us at our deepest wounding. We are faced not only with outer contradictions but with some aspect of ourselves that we have not yet fully understood and cared for. We too are in transition between old and new patterns.

We cannot bear not being able to make a meaningful choice. Yet at the moment when we come to the crunch, we can fail ourselves. We hear our soul truth whispering but we cannot listen and follow. We may well be dealing with the area where we have most to learn.

This is why, at the moment I was about to start a new life, I turned around and walked back down the path I had just emerged from. On one level I was ready to move on, but on another, I had a lot to learn about my need to please and to be perfect, and burnout forced me to learn it.

Consider This: What do you do when you come to the crunch?

- Can you think of a time at work or at home or in a social or political group when you had a picture of how things should be or when you believed in something or someone and then the reality proved to be different? Perhaps you felt disappointed or disillusioned or disheartened or even devastated? Go with the first memory that comes to mind.

- Imagine that you are standing outside that memory picture and looking at yourself. How do you look and act? How does the someone or something that disappointed or disillusioned you seem?

- Step inside the picture to be your past self. Breathe into being this person you were. How do you feel? What are you aware of? Go behind the surface feelings and find out your deepest feelings and awarenesses. What was it that you expected or thought that now feels betrayed? What is the worst thing about it? Is this feeling a familiar one?

- Step back out of the picture, observe it again from the outside, and reflect. What was at stake for you? What did you actually do? Can you see another choice now?

- Can you think of another time when your pictures and your reality didn't meet and you reacted very differently? Again, go with the first memory that comes to mind. Can you see how and why these situations had different effects on you?

- Do either of these situations, or a similar one, have anything to do with your burning out? If so, make sure that you are as conscious as possible of what is happening in you and around you, so that you can deal with it in the best possible way.

Finally: We won't get it right

It seems that both at work and at home, the gap between our vision and reality grows larger and the confusion, conflict, stress and dis-illusionment greater. If we don't know how to deal with this, burnout is one solution. If we learn how, we can move towards a new relationship to ourselves and to our lives. It may require the first symptoms of burnout for us to figure out that there is something new to learn.

Whatever we do, we must have the humility to recognize that we won't get it 'right'. The story of being human emerges in each telling. There isn't a manual someone neglected to give us, a pre-existing story with a happy ending that we need to discover, or a viable future to walk into.

We can only choose to be more truly ourselves. The way forward is in our own bodies and souls and in our ability to find our truth day by day and hour by hour. This includes honouring our wounding and our vulnerability as well as our strength and our power. True freedom is a long haul.

In doing all this, we are contributing not only to our own evolution but to the evolution in the present understanding of what it means to be human. Those of us who have learnt the lessons of burnout are not only happier in ourselves, but represent a potential for change for society as a whole. When we find our way, we will be able to offer a new kind of service, one that may have a powerful effect on the culture that has helped lead to burnout in the first place.

Sue Townsend's Burnout Diary

Sue Townsend, whom I met originally because she taught several times at our centres in Skyros, has been for many years a household name in Britain. She is the author of the Adrian Mole diaries that sold millions of copies around the world, as well of *The Queen and I* and a host of other books, plays, articles, TV and film scripts.[6] She is also a woman sparkling with charisma, warmth, humour, generosity, integrity – and fun.

Sue has suffered from a series of illnesses which include tuberculosis, peritonitis, diabetes, a heart attack, a serious back problem and now near-blindness. Illnesses may have many causes, but Sue considers hers to be forms of burnout. Each of these illnesses coincided with a major stress period in her life. Often these were periods of great success in the eyes of the world. But in her view, they involved *'big high-profile work projects where I felt I compromised the work and I was really angry and resentful'*. At times she talked of these experiences in a way that reminded me of a proud mother lion holding on to her cubs while hunters try to grab them away. At other times, she felt as if she herself was the dead animal being torn apart for her meat.

Thus, Sue was continually coming up against that clash between idealistic visions and the reality of the social world. Each time, Sue's response was the typical burnout one of putting her head down and working harder until an illness stopped her in her tracks.

Part of the conflict Sue faced was the disjunction between being successful and staying identified with her class and her family background. To be successful meant that you were considered middleclass. This went against her left-wing politics and her nature. Yet the solution of trying to ignore the positive fruits of success and make believe it wasn't happening only left her struggling with those aspects of it that she couldn't avoid – all the ways she was besieged, exploited, envied and misunderstood by those who used or valued her fame more than she did. It was difficult for her to find a way forward that honoured her truth.

Sue's need to negotiate the effects of this huge public success and of fame, and her own enormous care for others, coupled with almost none for herself, throws the whole process of burnout into relief. But her attitudes and ways of driving herself, her difficulties in saying no, and the factors leading to her burnout are, in essence, very similar to those of the burnout people I have known.

Typically, Sue started off with high energy and enthusiasm, met a disillusioning reality, and then battled to hold on tight even though her heart had gone out of the situation. During the run-up to burnout she was divided against herself, denying her anger and resentment, not taking care of herself, over-riding serious physical symptoms, and working even harder than usual to produce the goods. To put it another way, her soul was whispering, but she was not listening. This is a classic burnout scenario.

Sue's repeated illnesses demonstrate a resistance to taking responsibility for her own health and happiness related in part to her personal and social wounding. Most burnout people have a similar resistance. But equally Sue's story can be seen as an expression of the way a remarkable woman is being challenged again and again by her destiny to take a step forward. It is a reminder to all of us to honour our own struggles as a contribution to the evolutionary process we are all going through.

Sue sees her illnesses as a series of burnout experiences in which her old personality got diminished by the fire that 'destroys, cleanses, and sometimes renews'. She believes that each time, she built herself up from a very low point and progressively became stronger, more honest and happier. *resilience.*

Sue age twenty-three

I had tuberculosis of the stomach when I was twenty-three and I was very ill and that coincided with my first husband leaving me. My doctors concluded that the only possible reason for me having tuberculosis was that it had been caused by stress, which was the first time I think I'd heard stress being used in connection with illness.

Sue had, as it turned out, both peritonitis and tuberculosis, and spent Christmas in hospital.

Her marriage had always been bad, and she had three small children and almost no money. She read secretly and wrote secretly, as her husband didn't like her reading and never knew she was writing. And she gave to everyone, to her family, to friends, to neighbours and to strangers on the bus. But there was no concern for herself.

I felt nothing about my own welfare. That was never a considera-tion. I would never have been able to say to someone – 'I'm tired, I'm going to lie down now.' That wasn't ever in the picture.

I closed down, I only showed a quarter of what I was feeling. The stress was too high. It would have been the equivalent of Vesuvius erupting. I was giving hugely to everybody, including my husband – doing everything he asked me to do, becoming the person he wanted me to be – but I obviously couldn't do that wholly. I had my own life going on inside my head.

Although she gave and gave in a bad situation, and without self-care, she continued full of energy until her husband started having an affair. At this point, she lost heart. The flow between them had been disrupted and she could no longer be fed by the relationship. She was not only sad but also highly anxious, depressed and angry, yet she expressed none of these feelings and just kept going.

I did feel them but I didn't know how to express them. I didn't want other people to know how badly I felt.

Sue couldn't leave her husband when she found he was having an affair, partly because she had neither money nor a place to go. At that time, working-class women with small children didn't consider leaving their husbands. But also, she still loved him and needed him emotionally. So she was in denial, divided against herself and unable to stop and make a rational decision to protect herself:

And anyway, I loved him. I wouldn't now call it love. But I called it love at the time. I heard women on the Jerry Springer show saying when asked why they didn't leave their husbands who abused them, 'Because I loved him, Jerry.' It was the love of the lion for the lion tamer; it needs him for food.

When I asked her to imagine being in the body of that person she was in the period leading up to her illness, this was what she saw.

A woman who had six items of clothing – two blouses, two skirts and a coat, and obviously underwear. One set would be in the wash and one set worn. That's how little I had. I'm a kind of robot with a big smile.

My head was never easy, I had a kind of fuzzy brain. It was filled with anxiety, like lightning sending one anxious thought after another, a whole head full of lightning flashes. I lived in a state of high anxiety, constantly, almost like an animal that was constantly being hunted, eventually even in my sleep.

The nearest I got to admitting it was to ask people the question, 'If you won a lot of money on the football pools what would you do with it?' If they asked me what I wanted, I'd say, 'All I want is peace of mind.' It was like a code to say I was in trouble. I wanted my head cleared.

The illness happened about a month after I found out he was having an affair, and there was a period of him leaving and coming back and it was during a time when he was away that I finally got ill. I probably hadn't been eating or sleeping or caring about myself at all.

Life became intolerable, and it was a relief when I went into hospital. I just remember the wonderful comfort of lying in a hospital bed and not doing anything.

Sue aged thirty-six to thirty-nine

At the age of thirty-six Sue was diagnosed with diabetes. By now she was married again, this time happily. In the period leading up to the illness her Adrian Mole books became a runaway success and she was desperately trying to fight the implications of this success.

That was at the peak of the whole Mole thing – that Mole Mania. It was just gigantic. It had been at the top of the best-selling list for years, selling millions and millions of copies, here and in translation throughout the world. It all seemed unreal to me. I was trying to be more ordinary than ordinary, overcompensating like mad, especially with the children – baking bread and making homemade Christmas decorations and we all sat down to dinner and we had three courses. I wasn't gracefully accepting success and dealing with it and enjoying it. I was refusing to enjoy it because that would have set me apart. It was like living three busy lives – the writer, the mother and wife – and the other one – me.

Getting diabetes was a health turning-point because it demands a strict health regime and makes you vulnerable to other illnesses, particularly if you don't care for your health. Sue didn't. Things got worse as more and more was demanded of her from all sides and she struggled to meet all these demands. Often she was feeling angry and abused by what was happening but doing it anyway. Three years later she had a heart attack.

It was near the end of a huge amount of work. I was working on a drama series that I actually didn't like: I was working with other people and I got too far in and couldn't get out and felt obliged to finish it. I was also writing a book, as well as getting an enormous amount of publicity, and an enormous number of requests to open things, close things, give money to charity. Strangers wrote begging letters asking for help with very heartbreaking stories. Dying children always seemed to occur in these letters, quite a few of them wanting to go to Disneyland before they died. Also people I knew wrote to me and asked me for money – old schoolfriends, some distant relations – and every day there would be a huge pile of letters from strangers, not all asking for money, but most people asking for something.

And I just felt like a big corpse which was getting nibbled away, getting devoured by rodents. Everybody wanted a piece of me. I didn't think they thought of me as a person. They saw me as a lump of meat, and they were more interested in their piece of me than they were of me as a whole living body.

In her work, too, she allowed herself to be bullied.

The process of rehearsal for a writer, either for television or theatre, can be a very disheartening process. You can be bullied by directors and by actors, and I used to give in constantly even though I knew what they were suggesting was inferior.

Despite this sense of being abused, she kept colluding with these attitudes, because she tended to have the same attitude toward herself.

I set no boundaries for myself. I did what anybody asked me to do. I also got huge amounts of offers of work, so I was constantly over-commissioned. I was always working on two or three quite large projects. And I was hardly sleeping. It was common for me to work until two or three o'clock in the morning.

When I asked Sue why she wanted to do this, she replied:

I didn't want to do it. I didn't know how to say no. I just obeyed people. I kind of thought that they were requesting or commanding me to do things and I had to say yes. I had no self-esteem at all – and the more successful I became the less it seemed I had. Because it seemed the more successful I became, the more life seemed to be a fantasy I was living in rather than real. It was extraordinary and out of my experience. And I had never even wanted these things or looked for them or seen them as desirable.

She was truly unable to say no to anyone in the crucial area of her creativity to which her burnout relates, although she could say no to her children, who were never in that problem area.

I was afraid people would be angry and upset and disappointed, I would cause them pain at some point. I felt physical fear, extreme anxiety about saying no. Even writing a letter saying, 'I'm sorry but I won't be in the country to open your church fête' grew impossible. I couldn't bear for a stranger to get a letter that disappointed them even for a moment. The only people I ever said no to were my children because I wanted them to have good manners and eat with a knife and fork and not to wear their tutu to school – even I knew that you have to say no to children occasionally.

She simply ignored all the symptoms that led up the heart attack and kept speeding along faster and faster.

I had had angina for about six months before I actually had the heart attack but I didn't know I had angina. I had pains which prevented me from running, walking quickly down the street – doing anything particularly energetic – which I just ignored. I used to occasionally make little jokes like 'Jesus, if I don't stop doing this I'll have a heart attack.'

I asked her, to go back with her present consciousness to how she was then. How did she look and feel?

Speed. A cartoon character drawn on the page to indicate speed. They've got lines indicating displaced air. My hands stretched out rushing to catch the train, to catch this, to catch that, never present in the moment, always thinking about the next move. Inside? Hollow, but – sounds mad – but a kind of a head wearing a leather mask or a leather headdress that covered the face. I think it was keeping me in, stopping me from screaming, crying, saying what I truly felt, seeing the true situation. I was just doing too many things and also trying to be fully here for the children and for my husband and for my extended family.

If her soul was whispering now, I asked her, what was it saying?

Enough already. Enough. Just stop. That's all.

Sue tells the story of running a children's party for her daughter doubled over because she was in such pain, actually aware that she was having a heart attack, and then calling a taxi rather than an ambulance, and not asking him to hurry, and then waiting in a queue in Casualty. She never once used her extremely famous name to get herself any privileges.

And still, the work was all. She had no sense of her own right and ability just to live and enjoy life. During her convalescence from the heart attack, when she was under siege from journalists, she says poignantly:

I remember sitting in a chair in the kitchen – well, what do I do? How do I live without work? I didn't know how to live without work.

When I asked Sue if she had learnt something from her experience she simply said, '*No.*' Then she added:

I didn't stop smoking. I did take on slightly less work. I didn't take on so many commissions and I told my agents not to even tell me about work that was offered unless it was exceptional stuff. So I did slightly better but the work I did take on I still put in the same amount of huge energy and anxiety. I did that year stop even opening the mail. Even the letters from children I couldn't bear to open.

Sue aged forty-nine

During the next ten years, a number of factors came together which helped Sue to develop more awareness of herself and of her feelings. She also became more conscious that she could be loved for herself and more able to tell the truth about things she had always kept secret. But each time she opened up, she closed down again.

It was during this period that Sue came to teach in our Atsitsa centre on the island of Skyros. (She had been unable to say no to me when I called her late at night to beg her to come!) Our Skyros holidays have a community atmosphere based on a lot of openness and teamwork, and it happened to be the rainiest session in years and really required that teamwork. Here she was appreciated for her ordinary extraordinariness rather than her fame.

The important thing was Skyros. It was extraordinary. I felt good about myself, about my professional self for the first time, and as a person as well. I was instrumental in getting the polythene and lighting the fire and suggesting a bonfire and I also juggled my huge number of students I stayed up all night talking and had a fabulous time. I was released from myself. I'd been successful but that didn't stop people from liking me for myself. Before I felt I'd disappointed people because I'd refused to be this monkey wearing a crown, this famous amazing person. And at Atsitsa that first session, I used my skills – not many years before, I'd been working on adventure playgrounds, so I knew about nails, hammers, polythene bags, I knew about groups, I knew about the dynamics of staff teams. It was my skills as a person and a former youth worker. And I made real friends.

While each time Sue came to Skyros she would open up, unfortunately she would shut down when she got home.

She was also becoming more aware of how she was consistently turning down the rewards of fame.

The glittering prizes of success were within my grasp and I wouldn't quite reach my hand out to take them though I wanted them. I was afraid I'd lose something else – my family and friends, the safe people. I was always very nervous about seeming different. It was to do with people saying – she's getting above herself, she thinks a lot of herself, she's a snob, she's superior. That was massively important to me. And I was also loyal to my class. You can't be successful and working-class – I'm the disappeared one – you're immediately promoted to a different class.

What was the picture of herself she wanted to hold on to? Her poignant answer:

Part of the jigsaw of the family, one of the random pieces, not even a corner, just a bit of sky.

Another opening-up happened when Sue was writing *Ghost Children*, a serious novel which centres around an abortion. Writing this book was already a sign that she was becoming more honest. She began to face some of her feelings about the two abortions she had had years ago. She also knew she would have to answer questions from journalists about whether she'd had an abortion and she couldn't lie, so she had to tell her children before the newspapers did.

We told the kids. We sat at this kitchen table, me and Colin (her husband) and four children, and there were eight chairs. And then one of the children said – oh, there are two empty chairs. And they would be sitting here now. And it was actually one of the happiest nights of my life.

Then I closed down with my usual staying up all night reading or writing, and blotted it out.

Now, rather than just feeling like a corpse being pulled apart by strangers, her image of herself was as a Janus bust with one face facing one way and the other facing the other way. She had more sense of herself, but was still divided. Meanwhile, she was working harder and harder, with bigger and bigger projects, but feeling humiliated even about what others might consider a great honour – being called a National Treasure.

I felt a kind of feeling of self-disgust about the whole business of writing. It had got even more complicated. I had five agents. It was to do with people trying to edit the work and trying to change the work and to mould it into what they wanted, and in a lot of cases to cheapen the work. I was called in the newspapers a National Treasure, like kind of harmless don't we all love them, let's stroke their fur, like the Queen Mother, nice, harmless. It infantilized me. I felt I'd become this kind of soft fuzzy person and my work had been devalued.

She knew she had to make some changes in her life but couldn't do it.

I always knew in my head that this was not a way to live, but I didn't feel it in the heart of me.

This time the crisis came when she was writing and rehearsing her play, *The Queen and I*, with the renowned and formidable Max Stafford Clark. Again, what started off well became an experience in which she had to ignore her conflicting feelings and work harder. As her director tore her rewrites apart, she felt more and more angry and humiliated, but also exhilarated, and she worked unbelievable hours.

I worked all day in rehearsal, and in the gap between rehearsal and meeting Max I would rewrite, and then I would work with Max till ten o'clock at night, then I'd go to wherever I was staying and do more rewrites for the next day's rehearsal. And I would have half an hour or so of time off to grab some food, usually with Max in fact.

Normally, what kept her going was to have an hour or two off somewhere secret where she was completely anonymous. But now, as in each time of crisis, these secret recharging sessions completely disappeared. She ended up with an excruciating back problem, including severe sciatica and crumbling discs. All the doctors and specialists agreed that it was caused by her unhealthy lifestyle.

Once again the only way I could get relief for myself was for my body to break down. It was the only way I could get any rest without guilt, that was out of my hands. I'd never known such agonizing pain. I'm not entirely convinced that it was caused because I wanted it to happen but I have a facility to carry on where other people would have stumbled at, say, the third hurdle: I carry on to the winning tape with my legs broken, ridiculously neglectful of myself.

The story of the first-night performance, when she was in torment, says it all.

People dressed me, and Colin got a hairdresser to come to the house. I was bent over like a question mark. I was taken to the car and lay on the back seat. Because I couldn't sit in the auditorium, I lay across an armless sofa in the bar. In the intervals I asked the barman to pull me to my feet to stand me up against the back wall. When the audience came out I was standing there with a glass, in these high heels and a black frock looking quite good.

Sue aged fifty-four

Sue's back pain meant she had to let people into her feelings, whether she wanted to or not. And she was beginning very tentatively to be more honest and to take time out for pleasure.

I was able to say no, to show emotion and to stick up for myself more. A lot of it was Skyros really. I was gradually learning or being taught to be more honest, and people didn't fall apart or run screaming. It's much easier now to tell people the truth, to tell people how you feel. I think it's still important to choose your words, but even to say to somebody, 'I felt really angry when you said or did that' is so easy now and it would have been impossible before.

People saw me in pain with the back thing. I'm stalwart and have carried on and been very English about things, stiff upper lip, but with the physical pain which was so intense, I showed how I truly felt because I couldn't not do it.

I also remember having lunch with you, and Ari and Chloe (my kids) in that street in the sunshine, and that was just lovely. It was so unusual for me to have a day off. I used to even work on Sundays.

I was doing imaging sessions with her on the phone, because I was so worried about her. She herself recognized that she needed to get in touch with her feelings and her truth in order to save her own life.

The more true words you can speak, especially if they are uncom-
fortable truths, painful truths, the better I see them coming out as if
bile that is inside forms words, and it's like emptying out that bile.

But even so, she didn't really commit herself to a new attitude.

I was more assertive, but fundamentally I still had the feeling that I
didn't care if I lived or died.

The next major work crisis period came with the television series of
Adrian Mole . . . The Cappuccino Years. Again, what started off as
exciting and engaging her passion and wholeheartedness became
progressively frustrating and compromised because key scenes never
got shot, but she worked incessantly, sometimes for twenty-four hours
without a break. Although she began to have terrifying haemorrhages
in her eyes, losing her sight totally often for days, she fell right back
into her old patterns of neglecting her health in favour of the work. She
was, as usual, holding on.

I couldn't get out of it because I was holding on to my work – I was
trying to hold on to my script. I was trying to hold on to the truth of
the characters. I stayed and it was still enormously compromised.

While she knew she was at risk of blindness, she was reluctant even
to spare the time to go to see an eye specialist and almost refused to
do so. I remember practically forcing her to go. What would her soul
have been whispering now?

People love you and would miss you if you were dead. Be good to
yourself.

Sue aged fifty-five

Sue has now lost most of her sight but is undergoing operations to get
some of it back. It was an immense blow of course, and all the more so
because Sue's whole way of life was based on reading and on

observation of the world. But she is aware also of how the blindness, like the other illnesses, has forced her to stop and to think more and listen more.

In one sense it is a release. Because you don't actually have to do things any more. I have a big overall excuse now. It's as if someone has come and said – here, I'm taking all this away from you, this pressure to work, because you are registered blind, a guilt-free experience. And that card makes all the difference.

Unable to read, Sue spends more time thinking and listening to the natural world and to people. She also has to rely a lot more on the people who love her, and in so doing has found out how much she is loved and how she would be missed. As is so common with burnout, without her normal mechanisms of cutting off, she has time and space to feel the joy of just being alive and feeling loved. I asked her if she had more joy now.

Oh God, yes. Even the wind, the breeze blowing, and the sight of green which I can distinguish. I can see major contrasts. Just the sight, in Mexico for instance, lying underneath a palm tree and watching it waving about against the sky and also feeling the breeze is just joyful. And I allow myself to feel it. And also to know how much people love me and care for me. They demonstrate it all the time. My husband even, sold most of his business off and kind of nurses me, tests my blood.

She has continued to write – or rather dictate – articles, and is now starting a new book.

Who am I without writing? I'm nothing.

And yet she adds:

I am a much stronger person than I used to be. I'm content to be. I'm not conscious the whole time of how I appear to other people. But I am self-conscious about going out on my own, especially with the stick. And I've got that to do. I've got something new to succeed in doing. Part of me thinks that without struggle there is no life. I have less struggle in my old self, but the new self is about to embark on a period of struggle. It's a different kind of struggle, physically finding my way around and reclaiming some of my old life back on my own.

She finally feels she has *you have . . .* a right to take care of her health – though she says it is because she knows her grandchildren need her – and to find her joy. I noticed that stuck on her fridge was a post-it note saying in large black letters: SAY NO.

I know that I am incredibly important to all my grandchildren and I would really be sorry to die and to leave them and to have them lose me. So I keep my diabetic controls better, my glucose levels, I rest more, I sleep, I take care of myself, I eat better, I am just happier.

I allow myself to be happy. Before, it seemed like an indulgence to be happy, something flabby and indulgent and sickly. And now it seems – almost a kind of reversal – it doesn't seem extraordinary, just part of daily life, just the simple things.

3

Are You Burning Out, Burnt Out or Just Plain Sick and Tired?

Steps on the Burnout Trail

Jeff, Julie, Phil, Mary, David and Carol were highly competent, enthusiastic, energetic, talented and generous people to whom the following feelings, thoughts, and reactions came as a complete shock.

> *I was at work staring out the window and I realized I was gone. I wasn't really present. I was a ghost of myself behind some thick glass.*　　　　　　　　　　　　　　　Jeff, counselling manager

> *I was drinking too much. I wasn't sleeping. I was permanently worried. I got into conflicts with people at work. I saw very little of my friends. I became reclusive and remote. I couldn't make connections with people any more.*　　Julie, arts organization director

> *My body broke down. I was sleeping a lot and still feeling exhausted. I couldn't take a good lungful of air. I couldn't digest my food. And I didn't feel real. It was like being in a dream – everything seemed bright and the sounds seemed echoey.*　　　Phil, insurance broker

> *I was driving myself to carry on and work harder and harder but I was achieving less and less.*　　　　　　　　　Mary, airline planner

One of my clients phoned up in the middle of the night threatening to kill herself and I found myself thinking: 'If you're alive tomorrow morning, I'm going to kill you.'   David, social worker

I had run into a wall. I had nothing left. My reserves were empty. I thought I might be dying – but then I might at least get a rest.
    Carol, health consultant

These are some of the voices of burnout. This chapter gives a sketch of the profile of those of us who are more likely to burn out and summarizes why and how we go on the burnout trail, what happens when we do burn out, and what it is challenging us to do. I will also offer a soul perspective to help us consider what might be happening on another level. A checklist of questions can then help you to think about whether you or anyone you know is burning out or has burnt out.

Wherever the description veers from your own experience, please take your intuitive knowing seriously and adopt only what feels relevant to you. Not every person who burns out fits my typical profile. There are many reasons why we may take a different pathway to the same place.

My particular focus is on the individuals who burn out, rather than on the organizations or the situations that increase the likelihood of burning out, though these are also important. There is always an inner map that affects our choices, and we need to understand this map if we want to take responsibility for our lives. It is not our 'fault', but it is up to us to do something about it. There is no doubt, also, that some of us are very prone to burnout and have a great deal to learn from its lessons.

Those of us who burn out tend to be people who respond well to challenges. But when our heart goes out of our situation and we don't stop and reconsider, we become stressed, rather than stretched, put ourselves under even more pressure and soldier on in the direction of burnout or worse. If we are stopped by burnout before something more serious happens, it can save our lives, both physically and spiritually. If we listen to its message early enough, we can save our own lives.

The profile and situation of the typical burnout candidate

Those of us prone to burnout tend to start out as high-energy, ambitious and capable achievers. Whatever our calling in life, we manage to be the people who are enthusiastic, work hard and do whatever needs doing no matter what the cost. We often perceive ourselves as holding together situations which would fall apart without us. Sometimes this is true. Many of us think of ourselves as unlimited in our energy, even as 'Supermen' or 'Superwomen'. This is less a matter of pride than a statement of how our life requires us to be.

We are generally very driven and have a high need to be needed or approved of, or special. We often show a pattern of overdoing and overgiving without regard for ourselves. In extreme form, such a pattern has been referred to as 'workaholism' at work and as 'co-dependence' or 'loving too much' in intimate relationships. These patterns of over-responsibility are usually rewarded in the situation we are in, but may have begun when we were children in our families and felt loved for what we achieved or gave. As Jerry, a psychotherapist in the throes of burnout, put it: *'I started doing therapy at the age of five and started being paid twenty-five years later.'*

The area in which we eventually burn out, whether at work, with our children or parents, in an intimate partnership, in a social or political group or elsewhere, has two defining characteristics. It is where:

- We invest our creativity, our passion, our heart and/or our ability to contribute.
- We earn a sense of identity, value, belonging, purpose and/or meaning.

It is more common for women to sink vast amounts of energy and creativity into an intimate relationship, whilst both men and women do so at work. Of course, these are generalizations and may be becoming less true as gender roles and expectations change.

As long as the situation we are devoted to is working and our contribution is effective, appreciated or rewarded, we remain whole-hearted. Our energy is high and vibrant, and our life probably seems positive and successful both to others and to ourselves. But if anything upsets this picture, we become candidates for burnout.

Burning out

At some point, something changes either in us or in our situation or in the relationship between the two. Our heart goes out of our situation. There is a dawning awareness, often hardly conscious, that there must be another way, that it can't be right to continue as we are.

Some of us listen to this feeling and make significant changes in our lives – a new job, a new relationship, or a new approach to our old job or relationship. In this way, we stop ourselves from continuing on the burnout trail.

But those of us who keep going, denying everything that contradicts the path we are on, are likely to head for a major burnout. Driven by fear of losing what we had rather than positive intention, we are no longer in a flow with ourselves or with our lives. We cut off from our bodies, our feelings, sometimes our friends and family. We become divided against ourselves. Our head, heart and soul are not in alignment. We operate like a car with the accelerator and the brake working at the same time and the tank down to empty.

At some point we start experiencing the range of physical mental and emotional symptoms described in Chapter 1. If we don't take notice, these tend to get more and more serious. Jeff, counselling manager, described what adds up to a catalogue of classic burnout symptoms:

> *The person sitting there wasn't me. I wasn't really there. I wasn't enjoying anything. I felt like I didn't fit my life. I was in the wrong position, doing the wrong thing, and I shouldn't be there.*
>
> *I was definitely losing it at work. I started to feel more indifferent to clients. I felt angry at colleagues. I had a combination of anger, cynicism, hate and disillusionment. I was furious – hating myself and hating them at the same time. An impotent rage. I was also*

terribly exhausted, and started getting physical symptoms. I also begun to get more addicted to things, one minute chocolate, then drinking, then a phase of casual sex.

I woke up one day and thought: 'I don't know why, but I need to go to the doctor.' The doctor said, 'You're not going back – I'm signing you out.' He thought it was burnout and depression. My thyroid had gone wrong. That's to do with energy. I was so exhausted I couldn't get up or do anything.

Once things get this serious, we are well and truly unable to keep it all going. We may not even be able to get out of bed.

Burning out may literally save our lives by stopping us before we suffer a more serious or fatal illness. It operates like a circuit breaker that keeps the whole system from blowing. On another level, burning out saves our life by showing us how and when our life lost its old meaning and by forcing us to do something about it. We may not save our old life, but we can free ourselves to be more fully alive.

What went right

When we are burning out, it is easy to feel like a failure. Yet we are talking here of success stories, in the sense that we have given, achieved, held together and cared for the people and situations we have been involved with. What went wrong?

It is what went right that went wrong.

As in the case of social evolution, our underlying personal direction is positive, but working it out can lead us temporarily into conflict, confusion and burnout. The process of evolution is always uneven, with one part of us ahead of another. When our situation changes, it challenges these stuck places and old attachments, and we can temporarily lose our way. If we take a more long-term perspective, we will see that a wrong turning every now and then is part of how we recognize the right path when we get back to it. Burnout is one of those times when we take a wrong turning and stay on it too long.

Wherever something is labelled as a problem or an illness, we must

uncover the yearning that has not yet found the right outlet. Then we can help redirect its flow.

Thus if we look at the driven work and love patterns typical of burnout people, we will find in them an underlying yearning to contribute and make a difference. To redirect this yearning, we need to explore new ways of contributing that honour ourselves as well.

We all need to learn to love and take responsibility while being true to ourselves. On the whole, those of us who burn out have learnt to love and be responsible. Now we need to learn to be true.

The soul has its reasons

We have evolved far enough to have a sense that it is possible to take another step, but may not yet know how to do it. This is where the soul comes in. In a crisis, if we reconnect to our soul truth, we can find a way forward when our old personality doesn't know what to do. To understand how this works, we need to consider how our soul operates in our lives.

What is the soul?

Most people have a felt sense of the meaning of the word 'soul'. When we try to describe it, we come up with words like: our true self, our values, the eternal part of us, our highest and best purpose, our creative spark, our love, our human spirit, the part of us that knows, our essence, our being. In the following discussion, think of the soul in any way you are comfortable with, or just as a metaphor for our highest and most loving truth.

The soul, as it is generally understood, operates according to a different set of meanings than that of our everyday personality. The soul's meanings are more to do with being and loving and what it's all about and why things are the way they are, while our everyday personality is concerned with control, success, approval, managing the status quo and achieving personal goals. Our heart speaks of both worlds and can be a link between the two.

Acknowledging that our heart and soul are involved in our creative life is not just for caring professionals or idealistic workers for social change. Burnout is part of the business world and so are our heart and soul. Being connected to our soul just means that what we are doing has meaning for us, we care about it, and our sense of truth and rightness is behind it. We have some sense of purpose that goes beyond our own narrow ambition for ourselves.

When dealing with burnout, it is crucial to determine how our energy gets fuelled and then doesn't. Think of the soul as a large fiery light at the back of us, larger than ourselves or our everyday lives, fuelled and guided by something universal. When we are in a flow with our soul, this both energizes us and lights our way. Our everyday personality is also energized and directed by a flow with whatever is working for us in our lives. As long as these flows are working well, we feel fired up, we know what to do and we can accomplish extra-ordinary things.

But the flow with our soul and with life also raises the stakes. If our heart and soul weren't involved, feeling trapped and cut off wouldn't be so heart-wrenching and soul-destroying. The more attuned we are to our hearts and souls, the greater the perils of not listening to ourselves. We are like people who have got used to purer food and air and now feel ill when we eat or breathe food and air that once seemed normal. When we disconnect from ourselves on the way to burnout, we can't help suffering.[1]

The Great Yes and the Great No

When our heart and soul go out of our situation, what we need to do is to stop, acknowledge our feelings and the outer realities, find our truth and follow it. In other words, we need to live truthfully. We must say what the Greek poet Cavafis called the 'Great Yes' or the 'Great No'[2] – a Yes or a No in which we wholeheartedly put our will behind what we know to be true.

Even if we can't figure out what to do, we can just stop, surrender, and keep listening honestly to ourselves and looking honestly at what is happening. This reverses our pattern of trying to keep everything under control and to make things happen the way we think they should, and protects us from burning out. Eventually our soul will catapult us into a larger perspective which will give us a sense of where we need to be going, what choices are available to us, and what is really important.

Once we see the way forward, we can say that Great Yes or Great No and take our next step. By expanding, we turn a situation that stresses us because we cannot cope with it into one that stretches us because it challenges us to find that bigger picture.

Jurgen, a writer, told me how he got propelled into taking a larger perspective on his life after he achieved success as a Hollywood scriptwriter. He was finding that instead of enjoying life more when he became successful, he was taking on all the work he was offered and feeling more and more hectic, stressed and overburdened. He ignored these feelings and just kept going. Then two things forced him to stop. While he was away working in London, his house burnt down, complete with all the possessions he had begun to accumulate as part of his success. Then, on his return to California, he developed a life-threatening thrombosis.

Having your house burn down is rather more literal than the usual burnout, particularly since Jurgen wasn't there at the time so he had nothing to do with it. Nor is it clear that his illness was a result of stress. But I have noticed that at a time when we are burning out, occurrences like break-ins or fires or muggings or accidents or illnesses often seem more than chance and are perceived as messages from the soul. Jurgen himself thinks of these two occurrences as a burnout and as ultimately positive precisely because they were so shocking and pushed him to crisis point.

I had this doctor who was very plain-talking and he said: 'You could die from this if this blood clot breaks free. You probably won't but you could.' Not long after that I was lying in the hospital bed and I suddenly had this sense of euphoria. If I made it through this I could have a new start. Everything I had was gone in the fire. And I felt that appreciation of life you get when you thought you might die.

And that's when I started looking critically at my life. I saw it had gone too far and I had somehow lost touch with that creative expression. Then I decided to move to London and balance my time between writing stuff for the theatre, TV, movies and films rather than just episodes of TV series which is what I was doing before.

The fire and the blood clot were actually helpful because they were shocking moments that yanked me out of the process. The dangerous thing is that the process carries you along, especially in Hollywood where it is related to material things. It's like a current that pulls you along. It's only if you get out of the water that you can evaluate it.

The euphoria Jurgen describes is typical of the experience of deep contact with the soul. He listened carefully when his soul spoke, said a Great No to his old life, and a Great Yes to his health and freedom, packed up the few belongings he had left and moved to London.

Thomas Mann's novel *Buddenbrooks*[3] offers a beautiful account of the soul's attempt to catapult us into a larger perspective, and of what can happen if we don't listen. It is also a striking example of the way so much of what we learn through psychological research has been prefigured in the writings of great novelists and playwrights.

The central character, Consul Thomas Buddenbrook, is devoted to expanding the success of his family name and his hundred-year-old firm, and he succeeds beyond even his own expectations. At the point that he achieves everything he has ever hoped for, he senses that reaching the pinnacle of success can lead to an inevitable decline. However, he doesn't find a new vision to guide him, but clings to his old ways and becomes more and more driven. He starts to show all the symptoms we would now recognize as the classic signs of burnout, including exhaustion, inability to relax, insomnia, loss of appetite, constant worries and fears, chronic anger, minor illnesses, increasing ineffectiveness and general joylessness.

Then Thomas comes upon a book of spiritual philosophy and has an ecstatic transcendent vision of universal life and love that goes far beyond anything in his church upbringing. His soul is not so much whispering as shouting to him. Like Jurgen, he gets into a euphoric state. But unlike Jurgen, Thomas repudiates his vision the next morning as his middle-class instincts revolt against his unorthodox experience.

However, now that a bigger picture has been shown him, he is at risk when he ignores it. Thomas continues with a shell of a life until one day he has a tooth extraction and then, for no apparent reason, falls dead in the street. As Thomas Mann puts it, 'Senator Buddenbrook had died of a bad tooth. So it was said in the town.'

Surrender now or surrender later

When, like Thomas Buddenbrook, we are unable or unwilling to surrender to our soul's guidance, our soul withdraws its energetic support for what we are doing. Sometimes we can almost feel the soul withdraw. Alice, singer and songwriter, talked of what happened after her partner decided to live and work abroad without consulting her, and she refused to surrender to what was happening and listen to the truth.

> *It felt like such a gross injury, like such a personal wound. But in that moment I decided I would do whatever I could to keep the relationship alive, and that meant giving away my power, not feeding myself. I needed to hold on to the magic, the romance and the fantasy of love forever, happy ever after.*
>
> *I feel like my soul retreated, and I have this image of me sitting among the ashes trying to keep the fire alive. It's a bit like my soul shrank away at the horror of the thought. My exhaustion came then from sustaining this relationship which wasn't a relationship any more, and keeping the myth of togetherness going, like keeping the home fires burning, literally.*

Burnout is what we do to avoid surrendering. Yet in the end, we need to surrender to the burnout itself.

If we reach serious burnout, we have to stop and then we have another chance to listen to our soul and find a new way forward. This is how our old personality burns itself out and our soul fire begins to light our way: when our old ways have driven us to collapse, we can reconnect to our soul and our emerging truth can guide us forward. Burnout is pushing us to follow our love and our truth.

We do still have a choice. Some of us notice our burnout symptoms and move on to a new job or relationship without having moved through to a new place in ourselves. We do not say the Great Yes or the Great No. This pattern is likely to repeat itself. Others of us just resolve to put up with the situation, stop putting energy in and be 'sleepers' until we retire.[4] Either way, we may not burn out, but we may also never get the lesson that burnout could offer us. If instead we choose Radical Healing, we take up the opportunity that burnout has offered us to find a new and more joyful way to live. This is what this book can show you how to do.

Stop and keep moving

There is an old spiritual rule that the soul doesn't care if we are in the light or in the dark as long as we keep moving and developing. Paradoxically, burnout, by forcing us to stop, makes sure we keep moving. We are forced to re-evaluate much of what we have held dear and to open up to new ways of seeing and doing things.

Our souls might not care if we are in the dark or the light, but *we* will. Being tired, miserable and ill is no fun. It is far wiser to stop before we are forced to. That way we can keep moving under our own steam and we won't have to deal with all the unpleasant and potentially very dangerous effects of the burnout experience.

Consider This: Are you burning out?

The earlier you identify burnout, the safer and healthier it is. How can you tell whether you or someone you know are burning out or burnt out? Here are some questions to help you work out where you are going in such a hurry and whether you might need to stop in order to find out. Don't worry about what it all means. Just tick the boxes if the feeling is familiar.

Do you feel or notice:

- ☐ Work is no longer a pleasure.
- ☐ Doing things for your partner or loved ones is no longer a pleasure.
- ☐ Pleasure is no longer a pleasure.

- ☐ You are doing more and more and accomplishing less and less.
- ☐ You are doing more and more and feel appreciated less and less.
- ☐ The list of tasks is endless but you're the only one who can do them.
- ☐ Your stress levels have hit the roof and are still rising.
- ☐ It will all fall apart if you stop.
- ☐ You are not doing as much as you should.
- ☐ You are losing faith in yourself.
- ☐ Everyone else is talking or doing things too slowly.
- ☐ You are in the wrong place doing the wrong thing.
- ☐ You forget things easily or sit and stare in the air.
- ☐ You have lost the plot.
- ☐ You don't quite know what you are doing it all for.
- ☐ You are doing it all for someone else who should really do it themselves.
- ☐ You are doing it all so that someone else will think well of you or at least not despise/hate/be angry at you.
- ☐ Whatever you do makes no difference anyway.
- ☐ You are tired of taking care of everything and everyone but can't stop.
- ☐ You are exhausted all the time and sleep doesn't refresh you.
- ☐ You have started getting illnesses when you used to be so healthy.
- ☐ You are often angry, frustrated, cynical and/or disillusioned.
- ☐ You've stopped caring about your clients/colleagues/family/or partner.
- ☐ You are trapped.
- ☐ You sigh or feel sad or cry for no apparent reason.
- ☐ You are detached from everything – no real feelings at all.
- ☐ You have an empty feeling inside you.
- ☐ You wake up worrying.
- ☐ You go to bed worrying.

☐ You hate. A lot. You hate people you love and you hate people you hate and you even hate yourself.

☐ You've stopped confiding in your friends and family. Nobody could possibly understand; anyway, you are too busy and have too much on your mind.

☐ You don't enjoy sex any more.

☐ You are doing or taking in more of any of these: drinking/smoking /watching TV/sweets/drugs/tranquillizers/casual sex/computer games/ Internet chat rooms/trashy novels/living in your fantasy life/your favourite escape route.

☐ You wish you could get out of here because there is too much to do.

☐ You can't get out of here because there's too much to do.

☐ The idea of getting ill makes you think longingly of crisp white hospital beds.

☐ The idea of dying makes you think you'll have some peace.

☐ You don't remember why living is cracked up to be a good thing.

How many ticks is a sign of burnout? There is no answer to this. Even a few can be too many if they are feelings that are new to you. Just look at the number and pattern of ticks. Notice if your alarm bells are ringing. Ask yourself when you started having these feelings. These questions are here to stimulate you to become more aware of what is happening in your life.

The deepest truth about all these questions is not on the surface. You could feel many of these things and not be burning out. The crucial question is: *Do you really and truly want to be doing what you are doing or being what you are being?*

And if the answer is no: *Are you trying to ignore what you are feeling and continuing to put pressure on yourself to do what you used to do or be what you used to be? Have you speeded up, stopped functioning, or begun to alternate between the two, yet not stopped to fully consider why this is all happening and whether you are on the right track? Are you on a collision course with fate, hoping you knock fate out before fate knocks you out? And are you attacking yourself all the while, telling yourself you are wrong to be where you are?*

If the answer to some of these questions is yes, this is where we come into burnout conditions. It is not the same as depression, nor the same as anxiety and stress. It is not the same as overwork. Nor the same as trying too hard to reach a goal. It is not just not liking your job.

It is definitely the end of a road, but the road signs do not give you any indication of this or you may be keeping your head down so you don't see the signs. If you don't stop, you may crash into a wall before you find out.

Finally: Too close for comfort

If any of this this sounds too close for comfort, you may well be burning out or at risk of burning out. If so, notice how that makes you feel. Notice also all the other thoughts and feelings that have been building up while you've been rushing around ignoring them. Allow the feelings to come in and just listen. If they feel painful, just keep breathing and keep listening. Don't do anything about them. Just listen.

These feelings have been knocking at your door for a long time. In the words of the twelfth-century poet Rumi: 'Meet them at the door laughing . . . for each has been sent as a guide from beyond.'[5]

And now, are you willing to stop this mad pace before you burn out completely? This doesn't mean giving up your job or your relationship. It means stopping the pressure to keep going in the old way, just letting go of all the strings you are holding, and resting in yourself.

Please do. You are dangerous to others as well as to yourself. You need to stop hurtling towards destruction.

Give yourself a break.

Save your life.

4

When We Were Wholehearted
What Used to Fuel Our Fires?

The word 'burnout' tells us of the feeling that our fires which once burnt strongly are now down to ashes. When I talk to people who have burnt out, I usually ask, 'Was there a time when things were different, when your energy was high and just kept replenishing itself?' Invariably they smile and eagerly tell me of how it once was for them.

What once fuelled those fires and then didn't? And was there some quality about the way we were fuelled that later made us vulnerable to burnout? These are the questions that this chapter seeks to answer.

When we were in a positive energy cycle, we were fuelled on many levels by the aspects of our life that met our needs and provided a channel for our aspirations. We were also wholehearted: we aligned our whole being behind our decision to do what we were doing, whether at work or in our intimate relationship. The unseen flaw in our wholeheartedness was that we tended to push ourselves to the limit with no awareness of how it was affecting us. This never mattered to us when we were wholehearted.

The way it used to be at work

Julie, the director quoted in the previous chapter, told me this story of how things were in her early thirties before she started a new job that didn't work for her and began on the burnout trail:

I loved my job. I was working hard as an arts lecturer for people with disabilities. It was artistic, creative and exciting. And there was room for laughter and time for play. I looked forward to going to work in the morning. It was rewarding and it stretched me.

Edward, in his late thirties at the time, was working as an engineer in the oil industry. He described many of the features of the ideal nourishing work experience.

There was a buzz to what I was doing. I was doing something worthwhile. I was working in an industry that required a great deal of conscientious attention to safety because people's lives depended on that and I felt that I was contributing to that so there was a purpose to which I could relate as a service. I had about twenty-five people working for me and it felt like I was doing something good, holding a lot of things together. And earning a good salary.

I pretty much felt I was untouchable and I could handle anything. And in point of fact the jobs that I was given to do were the most difficult, and I thrived on it. I was given impossible people to work with and I could get results that no one else could get and that fed the sense of superiority that I was invincible.

Many were led by a vision to which they were willing to devote their abundant energy and abilities. Janey, health consultant and editor, tells this story of how it used to be for her.

The reason I was doing that job was because I wanted to change nursing. I was trying to wake nurses up and get them to assert themselves and not be so submissive and to wake the world up and say, 'Look at these women, they are taken for granted and abused and exploited and expected endlessly to keep on giving without any support.' I was passionate to change all that. When I look back I am amazed at how much I did, and indeed have done until now. I was always a pretty high-energy person. Loads and loads of friends, busy professional life, busy social life, not much stillness in my life, a lot of energy and activity. Few boundaries between work and play. A lot

*of the people I mixed with were nurses and doctors who were trying
to change things, fight the cuts, improve services.*

Carl, whose story was told in Chapter 1, talked of how his vision
and his team leading energized him when all was going well. The
vision was profit-oriented, rather than 'idealistic', but it was still about
making a difference to his organization.

*I loved taking charge of the IT area and I had a powerful vision for
where this could go. In simple terms it was how a powerful
information infrastructure could transform the business, and it
could have a big strategic impact and gain competitive advantage.
So I had a strong, clear idea of where I was taking this and I knew
what the technical solution might look like. And I loved getting out
and sharing my vision and getting people hooked into it and working
with me in defining what would be required. During that time I was
fed by my job and it fed my confidence and everything else. My
energy was vibrant. I give out loads of energy when I am leading a
team and I get it back from that.*

Often, the boss or mentor played a major role in keeping us happy and
energized. Dana, policy analyst, said: *'When I had a boss who had
confidence in me I worked hard, worked at weekends, and never went sick.'*
People also got energy from the sheer enjoyment of much of what
they were doing. In many ways, work was not a chore; it was a
pleasure that they felt privileged to be paid for.

Not all of us thought of our energy as unlimited – perhaps because
there was always more to do than we could handle. But when we
looked back, we usually saw that what we did succeed in doing was
remarkable. Our energy must have been pretty high even if we
thought it should be higher.

The way it used to be in our intimate relationships

That abundant energy, creativity and enjoyment of being responsible
were there in intimate relationships that led to burnout just as at

work. Cara, an art teacher who burnt out as a result of her relationship as well as difficulties at work, told me:

I felt I had no limits. I felt absolutely fantastic a lot of the time. I was blessed with all this wonderful energy. I think it came from my upbringing because I was brought up in the country and I always felt loved and supported and understood when I was a child. I somehow felt I had more to give than lots of other people because my energy made me so strong. I had a very needy boyfriend but even being with him, I felt I had enough strength to cope with him.

Doris, an accountant who burnt out as a result of her relationship, described her sense of herself:

I was brought up in a strong family unit. I'm an only child. My parents have always been there for me and they are very strong as a couple: they have supported each other through anything they had to face and they are probably the most together couple that I know. And that sort of closeness is what I try to give in any relationship I am in. Usually I give a lot more than I ever get back because I have more to give than a lot of people have: I experienced so much love and support and still do now.

Both their relationships had an imbalance of giving which is normally associated with 'co-dependence' or 'loving too much'. Yet the literature portrays those of us who overgive as being needy and having a hole to fill, and ignores this quality of abundant energy and generosity.[1] All the burnout in the world never shook Cara's and Doris's knowledge that they were loving people with an abundance to give. Like many of those who burnt out at work, it was a shock for them to discover that their energy was not actually unlimited.

It wasn't always fun

Not everyone with this energy was doing what they loved doing. I have met many people who don't like their job or living situation and

freely admit it, but sincerely believe that what they are doing is right
and necessary. They do not lie to themselves and tell themselves they
enjoy what they don't enjoy, nor do they think of themselves as
victims or as desperately trapped. They do what they feel needs doing,
believe that they are the only ones who can do it, and somehow the
energy is there.

Barbara, managing director, told me:

> My mother is a manic depressive and was always having break-
> downs so even as a child I looked after her. I married a man who
> was a manic depressive though I didn't know it at the time. I
> brought up three children. Even when I was married I was doing it
> on my own. I'd be travelling a lot, had time for the children and for
> lots of friends. When my father was dying and my mother was in
> hospital for a psychotic breakdown, I had all the adrenals pumping
> like mad because I was pulled in so many directions, and because it
> was a crisis, I just had to keep going. I was coping, doing it all, plus
> running a business which was still very successful. I couldn't look at
> what I needed. I had this remarkable energy because I had to. I
> never questioned that I could do anything. I didn't think about it. I
> just did everything. I was Superwoman of the eighties. I was such a
> coper.

When something is truly necessary, all our doubts, fears and
resistances vanish, and we just do it. Nothing is too much for us
because we won't allow it to be. True necessity aligns and fuels us in
an incredibly powerful way.

The words 'true' and 'truly' are important. We cannot fool our
bodies and our deepest selves. It can't be something we tell ourselves
is true because we are frightened to admit otherwise. Fully knowing
that something is necessary and doing it whether we enjoy it or not is
energetically very different from the trapped feelings we get on the
way to burnout, when we hate what we are doing but keep telling
ourselves that it is necessary.

We can see this necessity power operating in wartime when people
give everything for a cause they believe in, or to save their own lives

and the lives of others around them. They may find themselves functioning at a level beyond the human imagination. Indeed, any important deadline organizes our energy in such a way that we can accomplish, at the eleventh hour, what would have seemed impossible at any other time. We are seized by the power of necessity.

We not only do what can't be done, but we may do it joyfully. Gemma, psychotherapist, who was in a life-threatening situation before her burnout said, '*There were moments of joy in the middle of it. It was as if the neurosis was burned out of me.*'

How love and meaning fuelled us

When there is a flow, our energy comes back to us in a positive energy cycle. What we gain in that flow takes different forms, from money to achievement to making a difference to an organization or to a loved one. But on some level it always has something to do with love or meaning. Our wish for a higher salary, for example, once it gets above survival level, is less about the money itself and more about the meaning of status and recognition, and being able to support those we love and are responsible for.

Love and meaning are the fuels that drive the engine of the will, that part of us that makes things happen in the world and in ourselves. They are also the light that guides us and shows us what to do.

From narrow self-love to universal love

Love and meaning can take many forms. They range from a narrow self-love and meaning which have to do with our own personal drive to a universal love and truth based on our connection to all that is. To put this another way, they include both the meanings of our everyday personality and those of our soul.

Ambition, greed, lust, envy, pride – all those familiar drivers – are powerful fuels, but they represent a very narrow form of self-love. They are based on a limited picture of ourselves, cut off from the world around us and striving to make it on our own against all odds, often by controlling and even abusing whomever or whatever is in the way. This may be an important aspect of how it feels to be human, but not the whole story.

The highest form of fuel is universal love and truth, which is the love and meaning that recognize our interconnection with all of creation, so that giving and receiving are happening at the same time. It is based on the understanding that we are not separate from other people, nor from the non-human universe. What is in our highest best interest is also in the highest best interest of others. It doesn't need to be expressed in giving to people: the enjoyment of the carpenter working lovingly with a piece of wood is also a form of this universal love.

Not all fuels are equally good for an engine or for the environment. The narrower the self-love, the more toxic is the fuel for everyone around, and eventually for the person being driven by it. However successful we may seem, if we are driven by narrow self love alone, the likelihood is not only that others will suffer, but we will find ourselves isolated and empty, wondering what it was all for.

Mixing our motives

When we look at how people who later burn out described themselves, we can begin to see how their fuel was made up. On the one hand, they had a vision, or wanted to provide a service, or worked to heal or teach or lead people, or took care of family members who couldn't take care of themselves, or loved the creativity of what they were doing. In this sense, their life and activity were fuelled by an inclusive love and meaning, even if they did not think of it that way.

On the other hand, there was always also an element of personal ambition and need – the ambition to be the best, the need to be needed, the desire for a good salary and a high status, the emphasis on being in control, the pride in having all that energy. Mary, the airline planner in her early thirties, described her old life thus:

I had this powerful feeling that you're in control, and you can control what goes on in your life and you have enough energy to do everything you want to do. You can do everything. I identified myself with work and with independence – financial independence –

being able to support myself – being seen to have a good job. Most of my identity was in my job. In my relationships, I was married but I was having an affair. The two were very separate in my head, which I find hard to understand now, and I would have said at the time that both were very good. Now I would say that neither was any good. But then I was happy with both, and with my ability to keep them separate. It was part of feeling proud of having the energy to do anything you want to do.

Escaping into responsibility

We can see this mixture of motives in the overdoing and overgiving patterns many of us engage in. Such patterns are often called workaholism and co-dependence. These are considered addictions, and indeed we are dependent on the personal rewards we get from our over-responsibility. Yet they are very importantly different from other addictions. Although they are escape mechanisms, they don't take the usual form of ingesting something, like alcohol, food or drugs, or engaging in a pastime, like gambling or shoplifting, or gaining something which may be at someone else's expense, like power or sex.

They are an escape from reality into a sense of responsibility for projects or people that we have a relationship with and to whom we give of ourselves.

The desire to love and to contribute and the sense of generosity and abundance tells us something about the level of our motivation that is to do with universal love. Both levels – the personal need to escape and the universal love – are true. It is confusing the two that gets us into trouble.

How wholeheartedness aligned us

If love and meaning are what fuels and guides us, wholeheartedness is what organizes the utilization of the fuel. Being abundantly fuelled is not enough. We have to be undivided and aligned behind our purpose. Otherwise, our system becomes increasingly inefficient, and challenging situations can become stressful where before they energized us.

Doc Childre and Howard Martin, creators of *HeartMath*, an approach to bringing the intelligence of the head and the heart into alignment, put it this way:

> *When a system is coherent, virtually no energy is wasted; power is maximized. Coherence is efficiency in action. Coherent people thrive mentally, emotionally and physically. They have the power to adapt, to innovate. As a result, they experience little stress. (p. 17)*[2]

Given the fact that we are such complex beings, it is hard to see how we can ever be wholehearted. Surely there are thousands of pulls on us in different directions, from all the various levels of our being, each demanding more of us than we have to give. And indeed this is one of the mysteries of how humans work. It does seem that we have an intuitive ability to line up our will behind something that seems to us to be of paramount importance, and to go for that above all things. This doesn't mean that it is the right thing to do, but if it holds, it will work.

This level of will is not allied with how we feel from one day to the next, but with that deep purpose that transcends the daily ups and downs of what we are in the mood to do. When I teach people about how to use their will consciously in this way, I say, 'Put your will behind the knowing, not behind the feelings.'

Sometimes this is the will of persistence, plugging on and on, dealing with whatever is on our plate at whatever cost, without question. Sometimes it is the dynamic will that sees a vision and follows and takes pleasure in the success of it. Either way it is positive and focused and it organizes our whole being to do its bidding. At its best, willing is not about making something happen. When we align our will, we instinctively surrender and know that we will do what needs doing. This is what it means to be wholehearted.

What worked?

These features emerge as fuelling our fires in the days when our energy was replenishing itself. Not all were present in every situation.

- What we were doing was of service, made a difference, or seemed necessary.
- We felt challenged and could meet these challenges.
- We had the power to effect change.
- We were proud of our own abilities and performance, sometimes to the point of feeling omnipotent.
- We felt appreciated materially and/or emotionally for our contribution.
- We had a positive connection to, or sense of community with the people we were working with, for, or on behalf of.
- We enjoyed the process of doing what we were doing and could be playful at the same time as working hard.
- We were wholehearted.

We were where the action was, we were good at it, it felt good, and we wanted to be there and contribute our best. Our highest creative efforts were inspired and supported not so much by our self-esteem as by what I would call 'soul esteem'.

Soul esteem is that deep knowledge that if what we want to do is right and in line with who we really are, we will follow it through and not count the costs.

We can honour our soul's purpose whatever our self-esteem.

What put us at risk?

Even though our life or work situation worked for us in so many ways, the fact that it led to burnout indicates that our fuel was already contaminated with a mixture of motives and attitudes. This confusing mixture put us at risk when something important about the situation changed.

Jeff, counselling manager, talks about how confused his motivation was:

I was very ambitious and I hoped and thought that I could change something for the better. I had a vision when managing the counselling department that this could be a wonderful service that could really make a difference. I really went for it. I was very driving. My belief about the world was that given the right attention, people will heal. People will change if you provide the best.

I had this heroic pattern of wanting to save the world and this steely determination to make it happen. And a streak of perfectionism. I wanted to be the best. I was trying to hold up a view of myself as someone who was powerful and brilliant, more than I really was. I was ambitious for myself and for the contribution. It was all mixed up together.

Jeff's 'heroic pattern' is common among burnout people, who sometimes speak of themselves as being Supermen or Superwomen. Many people have a desire to be a hero, but those of us prone to burnout often think it is a minimum requirement for being okay, though we hate to admit this even to ourselves. Heroism combines both levels of our love and meaning: the need to make a contribution, stemming from universal love, and the need to be the one who makes it, which is a narrower self-love, or what I will later be talking of as an investment. Was Icarus, who flew too close to the sun and melted his wings, an ancient Greek example of this dangerous heroism?

Ernst Becker, in his book *The Denial of Death*,[3] writes about this drive to 'stand out, be a hero, make the biggest possible contribution to world life, show that he counts more than anything or anyone else'. He emphasizes that it is our terror of admitting that we are doing this to gain self esteem that makes human heroics 'a blind drivenness that burns people up.'

Whether or not we thought of ourselves as heroes, our general approach was to put what we were doing and giving and achieving first, and everything else second, and not to look too closely at why we were doing this. This led us to that 'blind drivenness' that Becker writes about.

To sum up some of the factors that put us at risk:

- We thought our contribution was what gave us value, so we were willing to do anything at all for the cause.
- We put the needs of others or the requirements of work ahead of even our most important personal needs.

- We disconnected from many aspects of who we were. Other ways of being besides working, such as pleasure, relaxation or hanging out were not on our agenda.
- We believed it was up to us singlehandedly to save the situation.
- We didn't admit to all the levels of what was motivating us.

As long as a situation is good, it holds us, gives us meaning and value, and guides us as to what is worth doing and what isn't. If things change and we are no longer held by the situation, we need to hold ourselves. At this point, any contradictions in us really come to the surface. If we have little clarity about why we are doing things, and few inbuilt safeguards to keep us healthy and safe, our fire is at risk of becoming a forest fire that rages out of control and burns down all the trees.

Try This: How things used to be for you

- Invite a memory to come up of a time when your energy was abundant and you were wholehearted. You can just ask yourself, *When was I wholehearted?* and notice the first memory picture that comes.
- Look at yourself and notice how you look from the outside. Then step inside the picture and feel how it feels from the inside. What is firing your enthusiasm? What are you wholehearted about? How does this make you feel and act? Step behind the surface feelings to a deeper level of your being. You could imagine this as literally parting the curtains of those feelings and stepping behind. What do you notice? And behind that? And behind that? All these levels are true, not just the final one you come to. Then step out of the picture and reflect.
- Now allow a picture of yourself to emerge when you feel exhausted, stressed, divided against yourself. Again, look at yourself from the outside and feel yourself from the inside. What is different in the situation and what is

---

different about you and in you? Again, go to deeper levels
and see what is different. Step out and reflect.
- Which picture does your life look and feel like right now?
  How does that express itself? What in you needs
  nourishing and protecting? How can you do it?

Finally: The light and the dark

Given that we often feel so bad about ourselves when we are
burning out – and tend to be critical of ourselves at the best of times – I
want to underline the healthy and positive aspects of our old lives as
they were before we started burning out. On one level, it is true that
we had a lot of weaknesses, ranging from a desperate need for
approval to grandiose illusions. But, on another level, we were also
fuelled and guided by universal love and creativity.

In my own case, I can see in retrospect that no matter what it was
that drove me all those frantic and exciting years, what I did was still
pretty good and loving. I didn't go to war and kill people to prove I was
of value. I cared for my family, did therapy, ran groups and communities and created environments that made people happier. This
was so for all the burnout people I have got to know. They were in
contact with a creative flow, had a vision, were contributing, and they
cared for the welfare of others. This consistency came from the fuel of
universal love.

My view is that one of the major differences between depression
and burnout is that depression has to do with failure and loss, while
burnout has more to do with a profound disappointment in love,
meaning and our ability to be of service. The 'dark night of the soul',
according to St John of the Cross (see Chapter 1), happens only after
the light of Grace flows in and shows up our impurities. Equally,
burnout comes to those who love well though not always wisely.

5

How We Lost Heart
What Changed?

When Jacky, an executive in a PR firm, learnt that her father was dying, she began regularly to travel 400 miles to visit him. Yet she still managed to continue to work overtime at her firm, go to the gym and see friends. She felt proud of how she had honoured her relationship with her father and yet kept up her own life.

After he died, she returned to work, only to discover that no one seemed to care about her bereavement. On her first day back, she was asked to work overtime that weekend because someone junior to her had been incompetent. She was angrier than she had ever been in her life. But she swallowed it and did as she was told.

And it was only then that she gave up caring for herself. Rather than disengaging, she just worked harder and harder, gave up going to the gym, withdrew from her friends, and allowed her life to move completely out of balance. Soon she *had* no life but her work. She drove herself into the ground and burnt out. When I talked to her, she was having six months off work and was dreading going back.

This story gives us an example of a defining moment or trigger event that starts us on the burnout trail. The turning-point, surprisingly, was not Jacky's father's death, but the moment she swallowed her anger. The story also reminds us how overwork can be the effect, not the cause, of the burnout process.

In this chapter, we explore the variety of changes that can lead us to lose heart. In my view, for a change to lead to burnout there needs to be a pivotal point or a period when we are deeply affected by something in ourselves or in our lives, but we ignore or over-ride its powerful implications. Often, this experience evokes old, familiar feelings that we have never learned to deal with. When we push down these feelings and drive ourselves even harder, any confusions we had before will now split us apart inside. We are no longer wholehearted.

When we've changed

The change that precipitates burnout may be a result of a change in us. This can come about for a number of reasons.

Many of the burnout people I have worked with had been going through their own inner development and had reached a new point in their life when the old choices no longer worked for them. Thus Mary, the airline planner whom we met in Chapter 3, told me:

> I found a Centre for Healthy Living and was doing evening classes in Alexander technique, meditation, singing, which were starting to make me realize that there were some important things in life not just linked to what you earn and what car you drive. I was turning around from a very materialistic way of life to a more spiritual one, though I wouldn't have used that word. I met people who presented me with a new set of values that I liked. At the time the job became difficult I started an evening meditation class based on listening to yourself and finding out what is important to you in life, and that was making me much more thoughtful. Consciously, I was learning some techniques that could calm me down after a stressful day but unconsciously, that voice on the inside was starting to get through.

When we are changing and we even make a decision to start on a new way of life, something can happen that seductively calls us to go back the way we came. This is what happened to me. There is a saying that the devil sees if he can tempt us on the way to paradise. But a lesson learnt is a lesson learnt. We cannot go back.

Jeff, the counselling manager from Chapter 3, after years of personal and spiritual development work on himself, had changed not only his feelings but his interests. Yet at the moment he was seeking to change his life, a job came up that was just perfect for the person he used to be. He accepted it and this was the job that eventually led to burnout.

> *I knew when I took that job that it wasn't right, but I took it anyway. My heart wasn't there. My heart was in the vision but not in actually doing it. It was someone else's job. It would once have interested me years and years ago but I was beyond my sell-by date. I should have moved on. But I took it because it involved more money and a promotion and that was what you did. You didn't not take a promotion – that was the social conditioning – and I listened to other people rather than myself.*

When death changes us

Sometimes an old death not properly mourned or a similar traumatic experience in the past comes up to challenge the well-polished status quo. A course or a therapy session might bring this into awareness. Judith, management consultant, told me:

> *It was the death of my father, that had happened about six years before, which came up. At the time, I had suppressed all the grief. Now I went on a counselling skills course and some of the grief came out. That was the first time I realized how I really felt.*

Recent deaths, also, are surprisingly common during the period leading up to the burnout, as in the story of Jacky, the PR executive. The dying process of a relative can put additional strains on us as we juggle work, family, friends and lots of other priorities. But more important, death has a way of changing our priorities. Julie, who burnt out more than once, told me:

> *The trigger the first time was the death of a friend. This was somebody who was younger than me, who was a brilliant artist, who had struggled all her life to make something of herself and to make a mark, and not to do what her parents wanted. And she*

suddenly got cancer. And I guess it just put me on to a different focus. I started to look at the bigger picture – what am I doing this for?

Similarly, Jack, banking lawyer, told me how his father's imminent death challenged his attitudes.

It changed my sense of values on certain issues, particularly on the significance of the relationship with my wife and the children who are of paramount importance. It brought me face to face with my own mortality. We could be snatched at any time. My father had a year's notice. I may not get that. So it's important to build on our relationships.

As a result, while his father was dying, Jack desperately tried to devote more time to his family. He didn't want to turn out to be a workaholic like his father. But he did this by trying to be everywhere at once – at work, at home and with his father. He was workaholically proving he wasn't workaholic. The strain of trying to do the impossible and feeling that nothing he did was enough began to lead to burnout.

This way has come to an end

We are naturally evolving beings, and what was good once may no longer be appropriate. This is what happened with Consul Thomas Buddenbrook (see Chapter 3): by the time he reached success, he already sensed that the deterioration had begun. That way had come to an end.

We may have ticked off all the achievements we had in mind, and now feel we have achieved enough. Or we may feel our present path hasn't taken us where we thought we were going. Our financial situation may have changed so that we have new choices that might be attractive but frightening. Our children may have left home, leaving an 'empty nest' or 'a burden off my shoulders' or both. Other needs and wishes long submerged start tugging at us and saying, 'What about me?' What is called 'mid-life crisis', which nowadays comes earlier and earlier, can have some of these qualities, and can lead to burnout.

Sometimes a particular life-style worked during the right period of our life, and now it is time for a change. Gwen, geophysicist, described this process in talking of her work in the oil industry. Like Jeff, she saw herself as past her sell-by date. She described herself as being like a bag of spinach:

The sell-by date is stamped on the bag. One day that date arrives. I loved my work for years. It was like a cross between the military and an extended family. It was a group of bachelors, mostly men, and you'd live together, work together, socialize together in an intense camaraderie. The job had quite a bit of intellectual depth but was also an art and a skill and not that demanding. For seven years that was what I wanted and loved. Then there came a time when the life didn't work for me any more, not that anything changed in the life. It just seemed like it reached the sell-by date. I wanted to be more settled.

Evolution is catered for within organizations by our ability to move up the ladder to positions of greater and greater responsibility. But ladders only go so far and when we plateau we may feel frustrated by our inability to expand further. In any case, promotion structures only work well for people who are suited to that particular ladder. For example, there is often no appropriate career path for people who want to keep doing the hands-on work, like teaching students or working in a lab, that first attracted them into the profession. This means that either they are promoted to a job that doesn't suit them, or they get stuck at too low a level for their talents and aspirations.

Mark was a brilliant chemist who kept turning down promotions because he wanted to do the technical work rather than manage people; that was what he was good at. But as a result, he was unable to advance in the company and was constantly struggling with managers who knew less than he did about his subject but were a great deal more powerful. He got more and more disillusioned and hopeless and this was a factor in his burnout.

When the work situation changed

On the other hand, it may not be we that changed but rather the work situation. What had once given a sense of love or meaning no longer did. The boss no longer smiled with favour, or something unfair happened, or the requirements of the job became soul-destroying.

Thus Margaret, teacher, wrote to me:

A turning-point was when I realized the administration demanded a constant testing of basic skills in what I considered a very dull and boring way, and that I was to 'teach to the test'. This was compromising my truth, and I felt that my work was satisfying the system but not the kids or myself. It had nothing to do with growing or learning anything, but with what the administration needed for kids to pass certain tests. I was not able to do what I knew made sense and I was afraid I would be fired if I stood up to the administration for myself and the kids. I was also afraid of just doing what I believed in quietly and not complying, in case the kids wouldn't be able to pass the tests and would feel like failures.

People who are posted abroad for a while can come back to a much altered situation that destroys their sense of belonging or value or trust. Kate, management consultant, returned to the UK from Hungary:

At work, my personal culture had changed, and I found re-entry difficult. I had been working at a very senior level, only to come back and be treated as less senior than when I left.

Then I learnt that though to my face my boss was saying, 'Yes, she deserves a promotion for the success she has helped us get,' behind my back, he rubbished me to the promotion board. I was learning to be politically aware, but did not really know how to play the game. THIS game was against my personal values.

Alternatively, when there is a change in management or in the organization, and the employees are not brought in to engage with that process, they may begin to feel that they can no longer understand or control their lives. This is particularly disturbing if open communication is discouraged. Thus Carina, business consultant, wrote to me:

Things began to come to a head when I was about thirty years old and working in consultancy for a big firm. I had been happy and successful there but the company had gone through some bad times and was instituting a lot of big changes. It became completely unclear what the objectives of my unit were. And the aims that were bandied about by different managers not only represented too much workload to be realistic but were actually incompatible with each other. We were in a no-win situation: if we did X we were open to criticism on Y, and vice versa. Work gradually acquired a kind of mad, Alice in Wonderland quality. I tried to confront my managers but it seemed to have become inadmissible to talk about the reality of what was going on. It was implied that if you couldn't stand the heat, you'd better stay out of the kitchen. I thought maybe it was just me.

Another extremely common pattern is that of beginning to overwork when feeling undervalued or undermined, as was illustrated in Carl's story in Chapter 1. This is a particular weak point for burnout people whose typical pattern is overwork and overgiving in exchange for appreciation, effectiveness and success. When the rewards are not there, we work even harder. The gap between what we give and what we receive widens, so that recharging our batteries becomes more and more difficult. Mark, chemist, described this process:

In order to get the recognition I felt I deserved, I was working harder and harder and becoming more and more expert. I became a world expert in my field. A whole new plant in America was built on the basis of my discoveries. But I still wasn't getting the rewards. So I just worked harder and harder. By the time I burnt out I was doing the job of three men.

We are not always conscious of the association between our feelings of not being valued and our overwork, perhaps because we don't like to admit how dependent we are on being appreciated. Neither Carl nor Mark recognized what was driving them until years later.

When better is worse

Ironically, burnout can be precipitated by a success. Like any big change, success can be stressful in a variety of ways. The new job, though it is a promotion, may not be suitable for our talents and interests, or may come without adequate support or supervision, or may require us to find new ways to do things. Mary, airline planner, told me how her burnout began:

> It started when I was promoted to the job I thought I'd always wanted. I was very stressed about it and pushing myself very hard. What I'd done before was based a lot more on flair and gut feel and this new job tied everything down to financial numbers and I had to get the numbers right. I'm perfectly capable but it's not my strength or something I enjoy. But I got obsessed with it, desperate to make it work, desperate to make it right.

James got a fantastic new job as Head of European Marketing for an International accountancy firm with a great salary and a high status. But he felt uncomfortable managing people junior to him who were better trained and more experienced than he was and he had little or no supervision. He never made sense of what he should be doing or whether he was succeeding or failing. He worked harder and harder, feeling worse and worse, until he broke down emotionally and physically.

Like Carl and many other interviewees, Carol, the health consultant quoted in Chapter 3, was only comfortable if she could do everything herself. When her workshop programme became vastly successful, she was expanding it too fast to manage without help but couldn't and wouldn't get any. She travelled more and more, got more and more tired, became unable to rest, lost her enjoyment and eventually burnt out.

Jurgen, the Hollywood scriptwriter we met in Chapter 3, summed up a few more of the hidden challenges that come with success:

The thing about Hollywood is that there are such highs and lows, it is really an exaggerated version of real life. People can get hugely successful in financial terms – and also fame if you are an actor. When people get to that level they don't know how to handle it. There's the fear that maybe this will be taken away from you because all around you you see this is happening. And the other thing is that feeling that you don't really deserve this – I'm a fraud and someone's really going to find out. And the third thing is the illusions you have about what it's going to be like, the idea that success is going to fix something about you. And it doesn't. A lot of it is about approval and if you are successful particularly in the acting realm you get massive approval even from people in the street. But you realize it is fickle. It isn't unconditional. It's based on how you're perceived, and you're only as good as your last film.

When the relationship changes

Burnout can follow upon a change in relationships either at work or at home. Relationships in the workplace are often crucial to our self-esteem. Our feeling that we have something valuable to contribute can depend on how well these relationships are going. Carl's burnout was largely to do with his relationship with his boss and his colleagues. And this was not his first burnout. Some years before, he had developed shingles, and the period that led up to it had similar features to that preceding his later burnout:

I developed new relationships with bosses as it went along. My way of managing life was to get intimate with the people that mattered. I needed to feel I mattered and was worthy. Each time the company was bought and sold, the bosses left and I didn't have that to energize me. Before the shingles, the division was sold to another company and the people that were there already became the new bosses. I was trying to get to know the CEO whose division was to go to America and I was really running like crazy to get approval, including travelling heavily. I was showing off a bit – and putting myself under a lot of pressure.

The same process can happen in intimate partnerships in which we over-invest and then get disappointed or feel unappreciated but keep going anyway. Marion, teacher, talked to me about her relationships with men:

> *I would see so much what the other person needed and if what I gave or wanted to give was too much for him or it was rejected, I would feel so desperate. I saw this so clearly when, at a time when I was happier than I'd ever been in my life, I met this man. I fought strongly against falling in love with him because he wasn't free to love me. But I could see so many areas where he was crying out for help and I just wanted to support him. Then my help was abused, and I started neglecting myself. I wasn't exercising, and I began eating badly and everything went out of kilter because I wasn't standing up and saying, 'This isn't working. What am I doing? This isn't honouring who I am.'*

When work or home is supporting us and nourishing us, the sphere that is working well for us can be protective of us, bring balance and help fend off burnout. But it is not uncommon for there to be a similar pattern occurring both at home and at work. Thus when Kate, management consultant, came back to London from Hungary, she not only was treated badly at work but was pushed out of her partner's home because his son was going through difficult times and had turned against her. This was when she began to burn out.

We may also cover up problems in one sphere by overinvesting in the other. Marion told me:

> *Probably the main catalyst to burning out was an abusive relationship, and then I would dull the pain by turning to workaholism again, so the complete failure that I was in the relationships didn't show up.*

When the contradictions show up

Sometimes the situation doesn't actually change, nor do we, but the contradictions in how we relate to the situation become evident. When Carl started his job as director of IT, it worked for a while because he was in the visioning stage; as soon as the movement to detail happened he couldn't manage without more staff. This was predictable because vision always turns into detail and requires a different kind of staffing.

Eve, who worked at an AIDS centre, described how her approach was not sustainable in the long run:

> *While the work was difficult, it was my approach to it that caused me problems in the long run. I tend to see EVERYTHING that could be done on all fronts. Unfortunately for me, I then believe that I SHOULD try to do all of those things. I worked on that basis for all that time, and inevitably, in the end, it all got too much for me. My body was in a knot, muscles all knotted. I cried over everything. I wasn't sleeping properly, and one night I woke up in a state of anxiety, with palpitations of my heart. I had the wit to go to a doctor next day, and she banned me from going to work for a month.*

We can get along without saying no for just so much time and then when we are faced with more than we could possibly do and still don't say no, we may reach breaking-point. Similarly, there may be something addictive about how we do things which slowly builds up. Sitting in front of a computer for too long can do this for us. Just getting too accustomed to high levels of stress and forgetting our joy can do it. We can go beyond our limits and not notice.

The personal and the social

I am writing this during the aftermath to the 11 September bombing of the World Trade Center, when a public event deeply touched the private lives and feelings of people all over the world. What is personal and what is social are never separate.

Resonating cycles

Our own evolution needs to be seen in the context of the evolution in our workplace, our relationships, our society, our cosmos, and yet we may be unaware of these interconnections. Janey, the health consultant and editor quoted in the previous chapter, talked to me about the day she was told she wouldn't be able to have children:

> *My husband and I went to the consultant at the fertility treatment centre and she said that we could carry on trying to have a baby but it probably wouldn't work. And even on that day I didn't give myself a day off; I walked into the office and my secretary said to go straight up to the boardroom. The managing director was sitting there in tears surrounded by other senior managers telling us that the magazine had been sold and was being taken over by a big publishing house. It felt like my personal destiny and my work destiny were intertwined.*

This seemingly chance event was, Janey felt, part of the interlocking processes in her own life and those of her organizations. She put it this way:

> *The projects I was leading or the organizations I was leading were also going through their circles of birth and decay. Like this magazine: I'd launched it and it needed launching again and that's not good for me to do. Someone else has to do it.*
>
> *I realized that I had to leave what I was doing, not because I was less effective but because the organization was at a stage in its cycle when I was not able to give it anything. I thought I could lead this organization to success. But I couldn't and I was destroying myself because of not being able to see that what I was attempting was impossible.*
>
> *When it goes well there is a congruence between your own cycle and the organization's. Any organization, like a ward or a therapeutic community, goes through a cycle – birth, growth, decay, death, rebirth. You need to know where you are and where it is in the cycle in order to know whether it is the right place for you and whether you can do anything for it.*

When we don't know where the change comes from

It is also true that changes may happen that our body notices and we don't. This is because much of what happens in our environment affects us in a way that is outside our conscious awareness.

People often discover years after they burnt out that there were all sorts of intrigues or secret negotiations or hidden conflicts going on at work or in their relationships. These had clearly led to much of their discomfort, yet they had no conscious awareness of what was going on.

How connected we are to each other becomes obvious in my Imagework workshops when people actually pick up the images of people next to them before anyone has said a word. One woman had an image of a sunflower, and the man next to her had an image of a bush with a sunflower leaning over it. One man talked of a washing-line that had appeared in his image, and the woman next to him said possessively, 'That's my washing-line.' I have seen images travel across the 'radar screen' of three or four people in turn. I remember one group in which out of seventeen members, nine people sitting next to each other had the image of being trees. No one else in the room did.

We need to recognize with humility that we do not know all that is going on in us and around us, and that when we search our memories for what changed in the lead-up to burnout, we can only find out what is at least at the tip of the mind's tongue.

Consider This: What about you?

- Do any of the changes I've described sound familiar? If you are burning out or burnt out or have burnt out in the past, can you remember the time when you started to feel super-stressed, depleted, empty, exhausted or angry? Was there a moment before that when something changed, inside you or in the world or both, so that you no longer felt wholehearted? Ask yourself these questions and see what comes up. If you did the exercise *What do you do when you come to a crunch?* in Chapter 2, it may be one of those experiences that comes up. If so, take this opportunity to go a little deeper.

- Go back to that point in your history, and watch yourself from the outside. How does this person who you were look? What do you notice about them that they don't know about themselves? What do you see is going on in the situation that they may not be fully aware of? Try floating above with your consciousness, as if you were a wise and loving being looking down on them: What do you notice now? What would you whisper to them if you could?
- Now, imagine that you are sitting in the body of that person you were but you have your present level of awareness. What do you notice about that person from the inside? How do they feel and act? What are they seeing? What are they denying? What is trapping them? If you could whisper something, what would it be? If your soul was whispering, what would it be saying?
- Ask yourself, and each time let a memory emerge: Is this feeling familiar? When is the last time I remember feeling like this? The time before that? Before that?
- When is the first time I felt like this? What decision did I make then? What did I really want?
- Step out of the picture and reflect. Is a pattern emerging?

Finally: When destiny speaks

We have looked at some of the changes that created those defining moments when we could no longer go on in the old way. Perhaps we no longer wanted to be doing what we were doing, or we no longer got the appreciation or feelings of competence and control that we used to get, or we were in a different cycle in our lives than the organizational cycle. Some way or other, it didn't work for us any longer.

If the meaning goes out of the situation, this cuts off the flow with our soul. If we are no longer in a good fit with the situation, the energetic flow with our lives also goes. Continuing with our normal pattern won't work now. We won't be wholehearted, and our ability to recharge our energy will diminish or disappear.

These changes seem on the whole to be chance events except in so far as we know that change is inevitable and what worked once will not work forever. But there is also this: using my creative imagination in writing that obituary when I was a young college student (see my story at the end of Chapter 1), I predicted the date of my burnout twenty-five years before it happened. At the time, I saw it as the date of my death.

This may be pure serendipity. But it may also mean that our destiny leads us to choice points where our soul is demanding that we listen and transform. I believe that my burnout was one such point. Perhaps yours is too.

6

Trapped
Why Did Fear Take Over?

I needed to feel needed, I suppose, and looked on as successful. If I let them down I'd feel so awful, guilty, and that they'd hate me, they'd blame me, they'd say 'It's all your fault.'

Barbara, managing director

I really needed to stop. I listened to the therapist and my colleagues rather than myself. I was scared. My identity was tied up in my work. My ego was at stake. How many would I disappoint? Where would I get my approval?

Margaret, teacher

I was trying to deny my own mortality. I wanted to work and race – I did a lot of racing – to challenge the idea of maturing or, I suppose, aging.

Jack, banking lawyer

My identity was based on the couple that we were. If I lost the couple, I would have lost a large portion of my life. That terrified me. I didn't know how I was going to live my life.

Doris, accountant

I kept saying, 'My time will come, my time will come when he is happy and successful.' I knew that side of me wasn't right. But I just couldn't help it. Being me and achieving something was tantamount to being selfish while someone else suffered or went without.

Cara, art teacher

These quotes by some of the burnout people I have talked to can help us answer a key question about the path to burnout: Why do we keep going when our heart has gone out of a situation?

In this chapter we'll be exploring how fear, rather than positive intentions, drives us toward burnout after our situation changes. A few of the images and identities we fear losing are reflected in the quotes above.

When we find out what is trapping us, we can begin to set ourselves free. We all have areas in which we are fearful and wounded and where we are holding on to something for dear life. The answer doesn't lie in trying to make the world all right, but in accepting that whatever the world does, we are okay. This is what burnout is asking us to do.

What are our choices?

What are our choices when faced with the changes that challenge our wholeheartedness? We can decide to transform the situation. We can leave the situation. We can change our attitude to the situation. All of these give us an opportunity for a new life.

Or else we can stay and feel trapped. This is likely to lead us to burnout.

Our choices are not always so clear or so conscious. Unconscious fears, worries and anxieties drive us so that we react automatically and compulsively. When we are driven by fear, we tend to keep everything going with what I call our 'control mind'. Our control mind is that part of our thinking that is oriented towards holding on to what we know and preventing what we fear. It is cut off from our body, heart, soul and real intelligence.

Our biological system recognizes the choices we are making even when we don't. Positive intention fires up the autonomic nervous system, while fear stresses it and leads to a variety of symptoms and illnesses. The different sequence of hormones secreted in each case spells out the difference between having a buzz and heading for a breakdown.

What is trapping us?

When we feel trapped, we often think that something external and tangible is trapping us – money, a pension, years of service, other people's welfare. But if we look more deeply, we find we are hanging on for dear life to a picture we want to have of ourselves or of our world, which has been threatened by the change in the situation. All the burnout people I talked to could locate an image of themselves they didn't dare let go which kept them going in situations that had otherwise lost their old meaning.

These pictures of ourselves may depend on our following invisible rules which make us acceptable members of an important relationship or web of relationships. The people involved may be living or dead: allegiance to long-dead parents or even ancestors can be a powerful driver. Often we see our role as accomplishing or achieving what they wanted to but couldn't. The idea of breaking these important bonds and allegiances can threaten us to our very core.

These images are also based on ideas we have about how things are or should be. *If you are good, then* . . . *If you are selfish, then* . . . *If you work hard, then* . . . *I should* . . . *They shouldn't* . . . *I'm not worth anything anyway* . . . *I'm not supposed to be happy anyway*. These ideas may not be conscious and may come from our early experiences or from our present situation or both.

The very familiarity of what we are holding on to is itself a background comfort. We go on with what we know, whether it works or not, when we are feeling too threatened by the new.

No wonder we cannot easily step back and reassess. We have too great a need to make things turn out right in the old way, and too great a fear that they won't. And this is unlikely to be the first time we have reacted in this way. Indeed, we may be repeating a pattern that began in our early childhood.

Too good to be true

I had the unfortunate idea that I was only okay if I was a good girl. My feeling is that it started at this moment: *I am about six years old,*

standing by my front door. My mother, upset and disappointed with
something I have done, says, 'But I thought you were the good girl.' I
answer her angrily and say that I am not.

Yet I must have decided that being a good girl is what would make
me lovable. My image of being a good girl? A little girl, dressed in a
white nightgown, coming down the stairs with a candle in her hand.
My heroine was Beth, from the novel *Little Women*, who was so good
that she died young, before she had to separate from her parents or
become sexual or aggressive. None of my female friends identified
with Beth. She is so goody-goody that she turned everyone else off but
me.

This image continued into adulthood, though not always consciously. I would walk around being wonderful to everyone and
almost glow, imagining others to be seeing me as that little girl with
the candle. As I glowed, I'd lose so much energy and get so exhausted I
could hardly do the angelic things that were required. The glow never
lasted too long anyway before I'd be forced to notice that I had ignored
someone's need, or that someone else was kinder than me. Worse still,
someone would imply that I was being selfish. A disapproving glance
was enough to communicate this message.

I'd wake up early, tossing and turning, ruminating for hours, trying
to prove to myself that I really was good, but fearing that I was so bad.
Then I'd go into overdrive, practically hurling myself against a wall, to
prove I would do anything for anybody and nothing for myself. I was
seriously, breath-holdingly guilty until I had proved my innocence
beyond a shadow of doubt to the toughest inner judge and jury in
town.

This 'good girl' image was life-threatening. Once, when I came out
of hospital after a not very serious illness and I couldn't get better, I
tried to find out why. Hidden in the corner of my fantasy world, I
found my old friend Beth and my unconscious belief: *Good girls die*
young. I decided – and this was a difficult decision that took all my will
– *I'd rather be healthy than good.* My energy came back almost
immediately.

This didn't stop that judge and jury from keeping a rein on my
life. One day in the middle of one of my inner arguments about

whether I was good or not, I had a simple thought that kind of stunned me:

But that's just faking an orgasm before God. Either you're good or you aren't. What are you trying to prove?

This thought turned my life around. I looked at myself closely. I was loving, intelligent, persistent, passionate, fun, but good, no, not good. I was just going to have to accept that. There was nothing more to prove.

When I told my friend Peter about this, he asked me who was 'good'. 'Mother Theresa,' I said. I was puzzled when he laughed.

Illusions are like weeds. You uproot them from one area of your life, and then they spring up somewhere else, completely unlabelled. Sometimes it was enough simply to notice that it was my good girl fantasy there driving me, and it would simply melt away. Sometimes I needed to send love to that little girl for herself, whether she was bad or good. I did whatever I could do to let go of that illusion – if I realized what was happening.

And yet when I was faced with my husband's disapproval and with the choice of either doing what was right for me, or doing what he wanted me to do, there is no doubt that my need to prove I was 'good' was what pushed me to burnout and I didn't even notice. I was lucky I didn't die young – or youngish – right then and there.

Defending our investments

All these pictures of ourselves that we hold on to are our investments in things being as we feel they should be. When we invest, we sink a bit of ourselves into something and leave it there because we expect a return on the investment. The return we want is not the 'thing' or event, but the feeling that we are okay or lovable or safe or acceptable, or that we have a right to be here or to belong.

It is natural to want or even feel that we need loving relationships or a nice home or stable familiar life, or money, or pleasure or sex. This only becomes an 'investment' in the sense that I am using this word when these things represent our identity, our belonging, our being of value, our having a life that is of value. It is to do with illusion and not the reality of what we want.

Illusions can affect us more powerfully than reality does, because our unconscious tends to see things in extreme life-or-death terms. Our dream images give us a sense of how fears become exaggerated. In our dreams, we are not just frightened or angry or lost. We are hunted by killers, or we burn down buildings, or we wander around in devastated landscapes. This is why when we have our identity invested in something outside of us – a car, a job, a relationship or whatever feels crucial – holding on will feel like a matter of life or death.

When burnout people I have worked with focused on their deepest feelings and described what they really feared would happen if they veered from their old path, they talked of being afraid the world would fall apart, or they would die, go crazy, be nothing, be of no value. Jeff, counselling manager, said:

I felt if I left, it would all fall apart. I kept ignoring the truth so I ran faster, worked harder, tried harder. Some of it was being terrified that my whole world-view would collapse and I would collapse or die.

Often these investments are entangled with the fears, hopes and beliefs of others who have expectations of us and for us. Challenging powerful old rules or leaving the fold altogether can feel like throwing a bomb into reality – which is actually the taken-for-granted world of our families, our work-places or our relationships.

An investment is always insecure. Even if all goes well, we fear it might not. We are always at risk. And because we are obsessed with getting whatever it is we believe our life depends on, and with making sure we don't lose it, we cannot just enjoy life as it is.

Investments are always about the future – wanting to either keep what we have forever, or to get what we yearn for some day. Often when a parent dies, for example, what we mourn is that we will never have the mother or father we dreamed we would one day have. It is one of life's ironies that the things we truly enjoy now are easier to let go of than those that are out of reach.

How we confuse love and investment

It is hard, particularly when we are in crisis, to tell the difference between protecting what and whom we love, including ourselves, and being driven by fear of losing a picture of ourselves that we can't bear to be without. Yet this difference is crucial. Love is giving, rather than investing, and it fuels us with positive intention, is unconditional and tends to be conscious. Investments drive us out of fear of loss, are to do with approval or acceptability that we can win or lose, and are often unconscious, rooted in our childhood, vaguely shameful. It is often not until much later that these unconscious investments become clear to us.

Now an arts organization director, Julie told me of her burnout when she took on an understaffed and underfunded role as Mental Health Services Coordinator and desperately tried to make it work:

I took it incredibly personally – I was failing all these people in the worst-served borough in the country. I thought I was the only one who could do what needed doing. If I didn't, it wouldn't get done and the world would collapse.

Julie believed that she was saving what she loved. On one level, this was true. But she later saw how invested she was in a role she had played as a child:

As a child, I was supposed to save the family. Really, I had to fight even to prove that I deserved to be alive. I was born between two sisters who died and I had two disabled sisters. And because I was the only one in the whole extended family who had gone to university, my father said, 'You're doing this for the whole family. You've got to do this for us now.' My father saw me as his son. I had to come home with that Golden Fleece or the Holy Grail. Otherwise I don't come home at all.

Julie's fear reminds me of what the spiritual book *A Course in Miracles*[1] calls 'losing what we never had'. That home she wanted to come home to never existed. She needed to begin to come home to herself. When she burnt out, this is what she learnt to do.

Recognizing an investment

How do we recognize on investment? It is an investment if we have a need to have any particular outcome in the world because without it we will not be okay human beings with okay lives. It often has something to do with being acceptable in and belonging to an important relationship or set of relationships. The fantasy of what happens when we lose the investment usually includes images of something terrible happening to us or to others and/or feelings of guilt, humiliation, fear or utter loneliness. We are terrified that we or our world will not survive intact.

These are some clues to look for:

- Our control minds become active.
- It is frightening to imagine living without these identities.
- We don't fully believe them anyway.
- We throw good money after bad.
- We get feelings of resignation if we lose what we invest in.
- We lose our joy.

Our control minds become active

When we are invested in something or someone outside ourselves and things go wrong, we are desperate to regain control of our lives. We think about it or them a lot, rehearse arguments with them in our heads, just find we cannot let them go. We often feel compelled to act, respond or retaliate immediately. And, of course, the more we try to control, the more it all escapes our control.

If I asked you to pinpoint where these thoughts are, you would probably point to your forehead or somewhere near the top part of your head, either at the front or at the back. That area is the seat of the 'control mind', the part of us that fights fear with more and more control.

It is my own personal rule that if a thought is sitting in my forehead, it is a defence against anxiety, worry, hurt or some other vulnerability. I assume I am feeling vulnerable and trying to gain back my control, but I don't take the content of the thoughts too seriously. Instead, I try to surrender and find out what I am really feeling.

It is frightening to imagine living without these identities
When we are heavily invested in pictures of how we are or should be, the idea of being without them can bring up all our unconscious terrors. Gemma, psychotherapist, who is still not completely out of her burnout, put it this way:

If I could just stop and let go, I'm sure everything would be all right. But it feels like if I do, nothing will be all right. It is too terrifying. It's like I'm trying to keep out of the abyss. It feels like if I don't keep going then I'll be completely alone, with no possibility of anyone, no sense that anyone even exists.

My friend Judith told me of how she sat in a meditation session and was given this little thought to focus on: *Let go of everything you think you are.* She began to name all the things she thought she was – her family roles, her work roles, the things she was committed to. She went through such roles as 'I am a sister' or 'I am a publisher' or 'I am a Buddhist', and let go of them one by one. So far, so good. Then she had a panic attack, and ran out of the room.

I sometimes call leaving our known reality 'stepping off the map'. Stepping off our map may be like stepping right into a big black hole. You can experiment with this literally: imagine standing in the middle of a picture of how you are and how life is, as if you are the main character in a play, or the central figure in a map of your life.

Then step off this picture, like stepping off a map. How does it feel? Do you feel free or frightened, or both? The fear relates to the investment. Just keep breathing and reminding yourself that these are just feelings and that they come from a long time ago. Breathe some more, and let them go. If you want to go a step further, pick up the map and throw it up in the air and see how it falls. Then step back in and find out how it feels in the new map.

We don't fully believe them

Ultimately, holding on to these pictures and stories doesn't do the trick. The fear of being shown up, and the determination to make sure we aren't, is there all the time that we are running our lives in what looks like a super-successful manner. This makes our victories hauntingly hollow. Thus Janey, health consultant and editor, said:

> I got loads and loads of approval and applause, and always had done in my career, but it felt like it was for me as the person in that role and not me, the person inside. I never really allowed myself to find out who that person inside was because it was too painful.

Similarly, Julie told me:

> I felt that everything about me was a false mask. It was as if all my life I'd had all these wonderful awards and achievements and certificates but I knew it was just pieces of paper. I hadn't really done it.

And of course Janey and Julie, like so many of us, didn't dare get out from behind the approval and the pieces of paper to find out whether people could – or already did – love them for themselves.

We throw good money after bad

When we sink time, energy and money into our investments, sometimes for many years, our identity then also rests in being proved right. Our fear of admitting that we may be wrong is what leads us to 'throw good money after bad' – both literally and metaphorically. We don't dare cut our losses and change our mind. One ex-gambler[2] put it this way:

> For me, the hardest part of quitting has been coming to terms with a single simple fact: the money I've lost is money I've lost. It's not

money I've yet to win back. It's not money I've invested. I haven't been putting good luck aside on the lay-away plan. There will be no redress, no redeeming hit.

This is particularly so if we have been acting in opposition to the advice or demands of someone else. How we will appear to others, or to our inner critic, becomes more important than what is really right and true for us.

For Elizabeth, alternative health practitioner, one of the most traumatic moments in her life was when her father and the man in her life pulled her in two directions, her father saying that she wouldn't be allowed home again if she went with the man, and the man saying she didn't need anyone except him. She chose the man, who went on to betray and abuse her, and she stayed with him for years, having two children with him. One of the main reasons she stayed, she could see now, was that she couldn't bear to go back to her father and say she had been wrong.

We get feelings of resignation if we lose what we invest in

An investment also reveals itself by the reaction we have if we do lose it, which is very different from what happens when we lose what we love. If we have to sell a car we love, for example, we miss it and are sad but we finally come to acceptance. A classic phrase from cognitive therapy describes this attitude beautifully: 'I am not less of a person; I am a person with less.'

But if the car represents our status, selling it means we have lost that bit of our identity that was invested in the car. We will feel diminished, humiliated, resigned, disillusioned, perhaps cynical. We will feel 'less of a person' than before.

Sometimes we feel both 'less of a person' and 'a person with less'. When we lose a partner, or a family member, or a job, we challenge not only our own expectations, but also the social pretence that such things don't happen. We may be surprised at feeling humiliated when we are bereaved. It is as if misfortune is a rent in the social fabric, and reduces our status. This is why when we have had a misfortune we may cross the street so as not to meet people we know.

How can we tell when we are feeling 'less of a person'? We may notice that we take less care of ourselves, or feel humiliated, or hunch over, or increase our addictions, or have bouts of bitterness and resentment, or begin to get ill. It is good to stay mindful of our own symptoms of resignation. When we notice them, it helps to find out what it is we think we have lost, as well as to resume our self-care again and support our sense of ourselves as being alright just as we are.

We lose our joy

The sum total of all this is that while we are so busy holding it all together, fearful that it will fall apart, our joy disappears. If we ask ourselves, *Where did my joy go?*, we will find that it disappeared at the moment when holding on to an investment became a matter of life or death. We have relied too much on love and meaning out there, and lost touch with the love and meaning that reside within. The only way to get our joy back is to bring the energy we have invested in the world back into ourselves and to remember that we are okay no matter what happens.

But what if it is true that we won't be okay? Every one of the people I have worked with who burnt out thought it was true, and yet when the worst happened and they lost this precious something or someone, they found that they were still there, and ultimately they were much more okay than before.

If we ask ourselves, *And if I stopped believing in this, how would it be?*, we may find that after the initial shock we breathe a big sigh of relief, the tension goes out of our body, and we realize how it would be: we could start living again.

Try This: A. Taking back my energy and/or B. Adult and Child

Taking back my energy
This little exercise is surprisingly powerful when we are invested in someone or something so that our energy or identity or power is trapped in something outside us. If you are

reading this book in a public place, perhaps wait till you have some privacy – you may look a bit odd the first time you try this. Later you can do it more subtly.

- Picture someone or something you are overinvested in. Imagine that your energy is like rays, or I like to say strands of spaghetti, coming out of a hole in the top of your head. The ends of the spaghetti are stuck in that person or thing.

- Once you've got that picture clear, then physically (with your real physical hands) pick up the ends of the spaghetti and slowly raise them towards your head, and then stuff them into you, as if into a hole at the top of your head, and then kind of suck and breathe them deeply into your body. Do it again if necessary. Try doing the same with rays coming out of your heart or belly. Or if you feel that the ground has been pulled out from under your feet, pull the energy back and suck it up through the soles of your feet. Breathe and come to rest.

- How do you feel? How does he, she or it look? If this exercise has worked for you, you will find that he, she or it looks smaller and/or further away, and you feel bigger and more energetic.

- Sometimes at this point, people feel sorry for the other person, who looks so weak, and want to give their power or energy back. In a kind of paraphrase from Kahlil Gibran's poem about children,[3] I say, 'You can give them your love but not your power. They have their own power.' It is not good for others to feed off our energy, nor is it good for us to be tied to them. As long as our energy is trapped in someone else, neither of us is free.

Adult and child
When you are in the grips of fears or other feelings that you don't quite understand and can't let go of, so that your decisions come from these childhood feelings, try this little exercise, which again is brief and can be very powerful:

- Ask yourself for an image of yourself as a child, a child who is feeling something like you are now. Even if what emerges doesn't seem like a real memory, it will be metaphorically connected to what you are feeling.
- Now look at the child, and notice what is happening for him or her. What is hard or frightening or upsetting for the child? Send him/her your love, perhaps saying something like 'It's really hard and I love you and will try to help' and give the child a hug in your mind.
- Having acknowledged and loved the child, perhaps still feeling your arm around him/her, come back and say to yourself, *Now, as an adult, what do I need to do?* See what comes up.

Finally: The abyss

Anyone who wants to be truly free inside needs to acknowledge where their identity is falsely trapped and slowly bring their energy and power back into their actual selves. But when we are burning out or burnt out we have no choice in the matter because our energy, our health, even our lives are at risk when we hold on to something we need to let go of and are driven by fear rather than love.

To reverse this process, we need to break rules that have kept us driving forward. Those rules are embedded in our culture and in our families but they are also deeply embedded within us. We are having to let go of whatever it is that feels like life itself, so that we can find out where our real joy will emerge from.

We may find that terror which Gemma voiced – that if we lose our investments we will fall into some fearful abyss. What is the abyss? Only those feelings that we have refused to allow ourselves to know.[4] The identities that we have created are there to protect us from an old place inside which is nameless, terrifyingly boundaryless, perhaps because we experienced it before we had words for what we are feeling.

If we look closely at the abyss, we will find a crying, screaming baby devastated or enraged by the way life has failed to meet her. We are terrified because if we acknowledge that baby, we may hurt too much or feel too powerless or hopeless or abandoned. And anyway, we are adults and are supposed to know better.

Yet if we faced our fears and stayed with the feelings, we would find that the baby knows a lot better. She knows she has a right to love, nourishment and the joy of being alive.

7

Nearly Killing the Goose that Lays the Golden Eggs

Why Did We Ignore Warning Signals?

One day a man going to the nest of his goose found there an egg all yellow and glittering. When he took it up it was as heavy as lead and he was going to throw it away, because he thought a trick had been played upon him.

But he took it home on second thoughts, and soon found to his delight that it was an egg of pure gold.

Every morning the same thing occurred, and he soon became rich by selling his eggs.

As he grew rich he grew greedy; and thinking to get at once all the gold the Goose could give, he killed it and opened it only to find nothing.

The moral: Greed often overreaches itself.

This fairy-tale goes a long way towards answering another question about burnout: why is it that we cut off from our needs and rhythms, go past our limits and ignore our symptoms so persistently that we drive ourselves into the ground before we take any notice? In this chapter we will look more closely at how and why we think that what we feel doesn't matter as long as we produce the goods.

This neglect of our welfare is exacerbated when the situation changes and we move more and more out of balance. We notice the dire state of the goose only when it can no longer produce golden eggs.

Valuing our golden eggs

This story of the goose and the golden eggs rings true as a fable about our society. The world is impressed by our beautiful golden eggs. Then it wants more and more of them and doesn't notice what it costs us. After all, the goose is nice, but the golden eggs, ah, now you're talking.

This attitude may be built into the ethos at work, or the rules of our relationships or the families we grew up in. Where there is high pressure on us to achieve or give, even beyond normal limits, but a limited respect for our values and our needs for empowerment, community, fairness and appreciation, there is usually also a higher incidence of burnout. These were some of the factors that changed in people's situations before they started to burn out.[1]

But for burnout people, the greatest pressure comes from their own expectations and tendency to drive themselves. The golden eggs are what make them feel worthwhile. The goose? Who cares about a silly goose?

Results are all

Many of the burnout people I have worked with actually had enough power in their working life to be able to determine their own work conditions. They admitted how often they didn't ask for help, or just did the job of three people, or held things together that should have fallen apart, or felt compelled to finish their work with no regard to any other aspect of their lives.

Marina, development worker, wrote about herself:

The Sudanese working day starts at around 7.30 a.m., and finishes at about 2 p.m. (after an hour off for breakfast at 10 a.m.). When I first arrived and there was so much to do, it seemed to me ridiculous that we should finish work so early and sleep through the afternoon. So I left the office at around 2 p.m., got home and had some lunch, and then continued to work through the afternoon at my house.

By August, when I went on leave, I was totally exhausted. I finally appreciated the reason for taking the afternoon off – the extreme heat is very debilitating and tiring. Nevertheless, even after I returned from leave, I continued setting myself ambitious work plans and really driving myself. Even if I was on a field trip, I would consciously keep pushing my brain to think about work and things I could do.

I was afraid that if I operated at the Sudanese pace, I would achieve nothing. So I pushed very hard – myself and my colleagues. It sometimes felt like swimming against the tide. I realize now that I set myself those targets. As far as I remember, they were rarely set externally. And as long as there was work to do that I regarded as important, I rated everything else as secondary, like time off and enjoyment.

Few burnout people had any regard for their own needs or wishes. Their main personal need was to achieve whatever it was they were achieving. As Mary, airline planner, said:

I was very ambitious and hardworking. I worked more hours than I did in the time leading up to when things were bad. But I had the energy to do it. I was kind of driven to do it, but that was how I wanted to be.

Sit down, you're tired

This memory comes to mind when I think of my busiest years: I was coming home from work, stopping to buy some clothes for my kids at the department store, when I caught a glimpse of an exhausted woman's face in the mirror. I suddenly realized it was me. I put the clothes down and went home to have a sleep. If I hadn't seen that face in the mirror, it wouldn't have occurred to me that I was tired.

All those years, each aspect of my life was something many other people considered a full-time job, so I assumed that I had to pretend to each person or institution that they had all of me. I did the best I could, organized other people to do what I couldn't, and ran from one place to another because I never really thought I had a right to walk. When my friend Silke said, 'Every time you meet me you are running,' I was surprised at her comment. I thought it was what everyone did.

Nor was there anyone around to help with this. My husband was too driven himself to notice, my children needed more of me than they had, and the people in every area of my life consistently felt they had to run after me to get my attention because there were so many other competing demands on my time. There was no one to say those simple words I never heard all those years: 'Sit down, you're tired.'

Professionalism

These attitudes can be supported by our concept of 'professionalism', namely, that when we are in our role, our personal needs have to disappear not just from sight but from consciousness. We exist only to serve.

Two days after my brother died suddenly, I ran a workshop without telling the participants what had happened. Many years later, I walked out of a hospital in which I had sat with the family and boyfriend of a close friend through the operation in which she died, and then went straight into my consulting room and gave a therapy session without giving a hint about what had just happened. I didn't want my clients to think I didn't care for them.

I finally realized how inhuman this attitude was when, during a break in a weekend course I was leading, I got a phone call saying that my father-in-law was dying. After hours of running the group feeling completely frozen, I decided to reveal to my students what was going on. I discovered that I could cry, be accepted, and then could help someone in the group who began to cry because of her own grief.

We can care better when we are fully present.

One of the group members spoke of how good it was to see my vulnerability. I said, 'What did you think I was: Superwoman?' Later I turned around and said to myself, *What did you think you were: Superwoman?* Yet this attitude was not so very unusual: it was probably the norm in my professional culture.

Janey, health consultant and editor, talked to me about how nurses are trained to deal with everything and anything, override all their potential limits and ignore their own most humane and caring impulses in the name of professionalism:

Nurses are expected endlessly to put their own needs second. They're at the front line of dealing with so much distress and pain and abuse, with no support to deal with it and no time even to do the simple, caring things that matter to patients. So they give themselves protective shields. In the long run this is very dysfunctional and alienating. It's a lot to do with why people don't care for each other within the system. When I saw how senior nurses treated junior nurses, how doctors treated senior nurses, how everyone treated patients, there was this cycle of abuse.

The black sheep

The classic burnout pattern is of being overgiving and over-responsible. Yet there are other ways in which the goose can neglect herself, and other kinds of golden eggs. Maya, a South American psychotherapist, talked to me about her experience of being put in a British boarding school and how she gained her sense of value from being the black sheep rather than the achiever:

Being seen to do well wasn't my thing. It was just being seen. I had a terrible fear of not being seen. I was always very active at school, doing wrong. I ran away from school, led rebel groups, did anything I shouldn't do. It was me not being able to bear to stop and feel. The only way to be in control was to be hyper and to act out negatively instead of positively. I went into overdrive. Every year I got the most penalties, and was known as the naughtiest girl in the school so I got some recognition. By the time I got to university I was seriously drained. Then I got serious circulation problems and that slowed me down. I think that was when I burnt out.

Giving away our golden eggs

Our golden eggs are our gifts. To have a gift, or to be gifted, is normally considered to be a good thing which gives us the feeling that we are of value. But it may not work that way. We may feel that it is the gifts that are valuable, and work hard to produce them for everyone else's sake, giving them away to whomever wants them, and yet never feel that we ourselves matter. Other people, too, may be more impressed by our gifts or our success than by our human qualities.

Possibly the most beautiful young woman I have ever met was on a course of mine in Skyros, and she revealed that she had never gott a moment's pleasure from her beauty. She had been taken over by man after man who saw her as a trophy and she had never learnt to say no and choose for herself. Similarly, a well-known actress told me that in the days of her greatest success and biggest awards, she never had a moment of happiness. How could she? She was working all the time to keep it all up and to give everyone else pleasure. The result was that she burnt out and only then discovered how to value being herself. Sue Townsend's life story (see end of Chapter 2) is, of course, another version of the same theme.

This way of living can begin in our early years. Alice Miller, in her book *The Drama of the Gifted Child*,[2] writes beautifully about the gifted children who are appreciated for their achievements at school or at home, but are not simply loved and adored just for being themselves. When these children grow up, they tend to alternate between feelings of grandiosity or profound specialness, and feelings that they are nothing and of absolutely no value at all. To hold on to being of value, they need to achieve more and more. This is a picture which is very typical of burnout people and is one of the things that drives us along on the burnout trail. Janey told me:

> My childhood thing was not getting enough attention and support and my way of getting it was being good at everything – being top of the class at school and being in the school play and winning swimming championships and being a high all-round achiever so I could tug the adults by the sleeve and say: 'Look at me, I exist, and look at my achievements.' And that was how I got my validation. I was still doing that at work.

Relationship contracts
Often the golden eggs are given away as part of a relationship contract at work or at home which is not spelt out: *if I do what I believe you want*

or need, then you will . . . love me/need me/take care of me/reward me/ appreciate me.

At work, the rewards tend to be given in terms of money or status or appreciation or a feeling of indispensability. When the contract is part of an intimate relationship, more common for women than for men, the reward can be feeling needed and appreciated. This means that the exchange can be very unequal. Yet we only begin to have feelings of disillusionment or resentment if we start to feel that no matter how much we give of our golden eggs, it is not enough.

Thus Doris, accountant, talks about how she helped her un-employed partner when things were still okay in her relationship:

We were a couple, so it should be something we face together. That's part of a relationship: if you care about someone you would support them through those sorts of times. You would help them when they needed emotional, financial support and you had every right to expect that help back when you needed it.

But when I asked if she ever got that help from her partner she said:

I don't think I ever needed it except for when I got ill and I didn't really turn to him because he was in a different country and I suppose the first person I turn to is my mum.

And indeed this had always been her pattern with men in the past.

I try to do what they need, and to bring them out of themselves, and what I need goes into second place. I try to get them to talk about things, almost try to replace the love that I think they haven't experienced with what I'm giving them now.

Doris didn't mind that, at least not consciously. Yet the lengths she went to in order to help her partner get a job seemed extraordinary even to her in retrospect:

I threw myself into getting him sorted. I was coming home at night and realizing that he hadn't even been out and bought a newspaper or if he'd bought a newspaper he hadn't looked through it. To start with, I wanted to take an interest in what he was doing, so I'd try to find out what he was doing to show it was important. It turned out he wasn't doing anything.

I felt very helpless to start with. Then I thought – well, if he won't do anything to help himself, I will do what I think he should be doing to help himself. At first I tried to give him encouragement to do it himself. When that didn't work I would do more and more for him. I didn't mind doing the job hunting. I didn't mind coming home at night going through the papers, looking for the jobs, and sorting out his CV because I knew I could have done that better than him.

In fact, she did every single aspect of the job hunting, except literally sign the application forms or appear at the interview. In her mind, this was okay. It only went wrong when he didn't do his share and she felt unappreciated:

What I did object to was that he hadn't tidied up, washed up, just sat in front of the play station. I didn't mind doing the things necessary to get him back on his feet but did object to doing everything else as well. I felt he was taking me for granted.

Even so, she continued to do it all until he got a job abroad, and then she went with him to find a flat and helped him move. A week after he was settled there she got viral meningitis and went to hospital. After she got out of hospital, but was still ill, she continued to help not only her partner but his brother. As with so many of us, it was a long time before she got the message that this wasn't working for her.

Did it work for her partner? Was Doris listening to what he really wanted and needed while she plied him with her golden eggs? Anne, a university lecturer who burnt out as a result of her relationship, said about all her overprotecting of her partners:

I finally recognized that no one was particularly grateful for all this service, and painfully, that worry and protecting someone is not the same as loving them.

If I do God's work I won't get ill

Our relationship contract is sometimes actually an unconscious contract with God or with life. Instead of directly taking responsibility for caring for ourselves and doing our best to meet our needs, we may believe that if we give our all, God or life should reward us in return with what we want or need. Thus Carol, health consultant, said poignantly:

I had this belief that if I was doing God's work, I wouldn't get tired, I wouldn't get sick, I'd be safe, I'd be happy. I was expecting the powers that be to do for me what I wasn't doing for myself which was take care of myself. It was a big shock when I started to get ill. Oh my gosh, I'm a lot more fragile than I have in mind. And why is that? After all, I'm doing God's work in the world. It felt like a betrayal. I did my part and You didn't do Your part. Your part is to make sure I stay healthy.

I filled myself with all that baloney, expecting that it would take care of me, and the truth is that no one is going to do it for me, I have to do it for me. I got that right between my eyes. I didn't even know I had that belief until this all started to happen.

Similarly Marina, development worker, believed that it was morally right for her to deny her own needs in order to achieve the good of others.

I burnt out because I had a very unbalanced view of life. Work was everything, and a way of forgetting or escaping from my emotions. When I reflect back, I realize that I did care passionately about what I was doing, and about the people in Western Sudan where I was living. (I am not sure I have ever felt that passionate about my work since, nor about making a difference.) But this was to the almost total exclusion of caring about myself. I remember thinking how self-

indulgent (and almost immoral) it was for my friends back in the UK to be discovering therapy and personal development when people in Sudan were struggling for their physical survival.

My attitude to work has changed dramatically since. I realize that often I was quite unproductive because I got so tired and pushed myself so hard. I now know that creativity does not usually emerge from that way of working.

Jack, banking lawyer, had the implicit contract with life that hard work and commitment on his part would automatically bring satisfaction and happiness. What he wanted most of all was a happy family life, but what he did was spend more and more hours at work. He thought that somehow, magically, he would receive the happiness he sought and felt he deserved.

The dangers of caring for others and not for ourselves

When we want the other person or the relationship or the work to be okay, and this is our only way of caring for ourselves, we do so at our peril. We can regularly over-ride natural rhythms of giving and receiving, of work and rest, of going out and going within, and endanger our health and welfare.

We never ask ourselves, *Is it good for me to do this?* but only *Does this need doing and am I someone who can do it? If so, I will. No problem.* Sometimes we are so out of touch with ourselves and our bodies and so unused to trusting what we know from inside, that we don't even know what we need and we have forgotten how to find out.

When others do not care for us in return, or the situation doesn't work out, we may just do more and more of the same and neglect ourselves even further. It never occurs to us that we can – and must – just let go of our expectations and take care of and appreciate ourselves. We have seen Doris, Carl, Mark and Jacky all work harder and give more, the less they felt appreciated and rewarded. So did I. It is one of the most common slippery slopes towards burnout.

Our willingness to ignore our own welfare can blind us to situations which are actually abusive. So can our tendency to value the point of view of someone else and dismiss our own. The run-up to burnout, when we become more and more frantic and less and less able to deliver the goods, is often full of unreasonable demands that we cannot say no to. When I asked Sue Townsend why she continued to give and give when faced with unreasonable demands, she said:

> *We just come back to the same reason – I didn't think I was worth anything. I didn't expect anything. I certainly didn't expect to be happy. It didn't feature as one of life's possibilities that I could ever be happy. I was giving to try to make other people happy. It was a mad cycle of giving and giving and giving so people are happy so you don't feel their anger. It's a protective thing. If I felt their anger, I would feel their hurt, and that would hurt me, whereas my own pain wouldn't. It was like anger by proxy. I've lived by proxy.*

Having a bottom line

If we are not to live by proxy, we need to have a sense of who we are and what our essential value is. This always includes having a bottom line – something we can't or won't do at any price.[3] This is difficult when we have a deep investment in the situation but unless we have a bottom line, we are open to abuse. We can always find a good reason to do what is not good for us to do.

Doris spoke of how she had a bottom line at work though not at home. She had been able to quit jobs that didn't work for her, but it was much harder to leave her relationship. When I asked why, she said:

> *Because all you have to do is go to a recruitment consultant and they get you another job whereas I'm not going to go to a dating agency. It's easier to get another job than another partner.*

If we have to kill the goose, so be it

It is easy to understand why, when the situation careers way out of control, we just don't notice or don't care. We are in the habit of thinking that getting *it* done, whatever *it* is, is more important than how we feel. *It* matters; *we* don't matter. If we have to kill the goose for the golden eggs, so be it.

This word 'kill' is not just a metaphor. It is not uncommon for people on the burnout trail, including Sue Townsend, to believe that what they are doing could kill them, to have fantasies of dying, or to hold an underlying belief that they won't last long, and yet still be unable or unwilling to stop themselves. Marina told me:

I remember an Imagework exercise that I did with you in Skyros, about the future. I was quite shocked to realize that I wasn't able to project into old age. It was as if I didn't expect to live that long.

Death or serious illness or accident was sometimes seen as the only way out. Carina, consultant, wrote me:

I'd fantasize just going and getting on a ferry to France or somewhere and leaving everything behind – which I knew I would never do, in reality, for the sake of my family – or having something happen to me like a road accident that would unavoidably prevent me from carrying on.

When I study the accounts of people who told me of their burnout and I look at my own history, I see there was invariably a series of warnings that we ignored and feelings that we overrode. Carol, health consultant, told me of hers:

I got so busy I didn't have the opportunity to refuel and I just went from project to project without the refuelling time in between. I didn't notice that my normal refuelling periods had dropped out. I started doing three or four projects in a row and at one point I didn't sleep all night.

Eventually, I found myself not able to sleep and I realized that I must be 'overtired'. I started having infections. And then in Israel I broke a small bone in my foot and then I had an ear infection so I couldn't even travel in the plane and I never cancelled a single presentation or a training. I just kept going. I came home hobbling and got sick again. Only this time it was a really bad ear infection. I just don't get sick and I was aware – now I get sick every month. I'm having all kinds of things. My heart's racing, I'm having an ear infection, I'm having headaches. I was going to work not feeling well and I was hating it.

Then suddenly last autumn I realized that I had run into a wall. I had nothing left, my reserves were empty. My body began reacting . . . adrenal exhaustion . . . my hormone levels went crazy . . . my immune system went down and I began having one infection after another. I could no longer honour my schedule and had to cancel several trainings.

Edward told me what it took for him to realize that he was burning out when he was working as an engineer.

I found myself walking down the street and there'd be so much stuff going on in my head, and I'd be having internal arguments with all the various people who were annoying me. I heard a voice like someone talking to me, and I realized that it was my own voice. When I was having my side of the argument I was verbalizing it, like an old character having a row with himself out loud. And it was only then that I realized I needed some help.

We finally became willing to take heed when we began to behave strangely, or felt so sick or exhausted we could no longer produce the goods. It was only when the golden eggs seemed threatened that we wondered about the welfare of that poor goose.

Me, greedy?

The moral of the goose and the golden eggs fable is: *Greed overreaches itself.* When I first saw this, I thought it wasn't relevant. After all, we burnout people were so giving, not greedy! Yet we had an important kind of greed, even when it was not, on the surface, greed for ourselves.

That greed showed itself in our inability to accept limits to our energy or our giving or our ability to cope with what the world threw at us. We could do it all and more. We could be everything to everyone. We could devour challenges endlessly. We could save the world singlehandedly. We could give our gifts away to everyone who wanted them or said they needed them. And in return for all our hard work, we would be super-special, super-successful, universally loved, even super-heroes. That too is greed.

It was this greed for super-duper golden eggs that blinded us to the value of the wonderful goose who produced them all.

Try This: Are you a goose with golden eggs?

- Where in your work or in your relationship life do you feel your golden eggs are more important than you? Does that attitude come from yourself or from others or both?

- Can you picture yourself in that situation? Start by standing outside and looking in. How do you look? Step inside now with your present consciousness, and notice how you feel and how others look to you. What is telling you that all is not well with you?

- When is the first time you remember feeling like this? Get a picture of an earlier experience, perhaps in childhood. Take the first memory that comes to mind.

- Again, picture that situation, watch yourself from the outside and then go inside to see how it feels and what you see.

- Let your consciousness float above you, as if you were a wise and loving being looking down on that scene. What do you notice or want to say from this perspective?

- Now, imagine that you can walk into that old memory as your present self and speak up on behalf of that child or the younger you. Do so now. What do you say? What happens?

- Go back to the more recent situation, feel yourself as that person you were, but then repeat the words you just said on behalf of the younger you. How does that feel? How do others look now?

Finally: Where the true gold lies

Once our experience of ourselves is disconnected from our actual self, the way we really are, and becomes dependent on what we do, give or achieve, we don't really know who we are, or where we begin and end, or where our true being lies. Nothing matters but making it all right out there.

Psychiatrist Dr Theodore Isaac Rubin, in his beautiful book *Compassion and Self-Hate*,[4] writes about the way we believe that only what we have and achieve justifies our existence. The truth is that our work and accomplishments are a function of us: we justify their existence rather than them justifying ours.

When I read this, I thought about the work I do and realized that what I do best is a function of being me, of my particular presence in the world. If I weren't there my work wouldn't be done, because no one else is me.

Someone else would write a book, run a course, start a centre or have children, and the world would go on. But if I am not present, my own golden eggs would not be there, because they are a function of who I am.

If those eggs are really gold, it is our radiance that they are reflecting.

8

When Something Is More Important than the Truth

Why Didn't We Say the Great Yes or the Great No?

Alice, singer and songwriter, told me how she cut off from her friends because she couldn't bear to hear them telling her she should leave her partner. She didn't want to know the truth. Yet all that time, she was writing the truth in her diaries. These diaries are a powerful demonstration of how we can shut ourselves off from what another part of us knows *consciously*, not to mention what we know *unconsciously*. After Alice burnt out, she went back to these diaries.

> *I had all this writing I did during that period of my relationship. And I always wrote the truth of my inner voice. Those pages saved me. I went back and I read everything and pulled together the threads of those voices that I hadn't listened to. Sometimes I went over and over a piece and I thought, why didn't I listen?*

Well, why didn't she? She wanted the relationship more than she wanted the truth. In this chapter, we explore how and why we, who consider ourselves to be principled, are actually dishonest with ourselves or with others at crucial moments on the path to burnout. We fail to say the Great Yes or Great No that would protect our health and allow the energy to flow back into our lives. We do not burn out because we have no choice, or because we care too much, but because we are not living our truth.

Saying the Great Yes and the Great No

At the moment when our heart went out of the situation we were committed to, we began to be driven by our fears to produce more and more golden eggs. As we did so, the pressure from our soul increased. We were being called upon to tell ourselves the truth and find a new way forward.

The way forward is a Great Yes to what is true, healthy, loving and real, and a Great No to what is not. It is a Yes to our true selves, and a No to what we think we should be. It is a real choice in freedom, a decision to create a space between ourselves and the forces that usually push us from within or from without.

Saying a Great Yes and a Great No doesn't mean selfishly doing what feels good no matter what the need is around us. Truth and love are both qualities of the soul. The more we clear our illusions and listen to our truth, the fewer blocks there are to our natural ability to love and to contribute to others.

If we allow ourselves to let go of other considerations and find our Great Yes or Great No, we tend to be flooded with great relief. Nancy, who left her twenty-eight-year-old marriage, Jurgen, who gave up a dream contract, and Bart, who resigned his post as a hospital obstetrician, all felt that relief. It didn't matter how much it hurt and how much they were giving up. They were living truthfully.

Nancy, international trainer, had burnt out more than once as a result of issues in her marriage of twenty-eight years, but she was fearful of leaving her secure life. She complained to me bitterly about everything that was hurting and even endangering her in the marriage. I just asked. 'What are you going to do about it?' She fell silent and stared at me. Soon afterwards, she left her husband. She had an overdraft and a suitcase and nowhere to go. But she knew she had to start her new life right then and there.

As soon as I decided to leave him, I felt full of energy, liberated, focused and fully motivated towards the future. I spent four months travelling and working abroad, which had been planned before, and I felt great. Then I crashed when I faced everything I had to do to find

a place, support my children and withstand my husband's criti-
cisms. After two months of being depressed but working to sort things
out, I finally felt established in my new life rather than in limbo, I
started to relax and feel happy again. Now my new life is starting to
flower.

Jurgen, the scriptwriter who left Hollywood for London when his
house burnt down (see Chapter 3), had to make another decision to
choose a balanced life over financial success. He told me this story of
saying a Great No, this time at the moment when he first sensed he
might get ill, rather than when he was actually confronted with a
crisis.

This company gave me the kind of dream contract where you got a
lot of money for an exclusive contract. I had always dreamed of
having a patron, like artists in the old days, who assures that your
material needs are taken care of. Of course there's a price – if it's the
Pope, then Michelangelo had to do the Sistine Chapel.

It was exciting the first year and I liked the people I worked with.
But in the second year, it started to feel like golden handcuffs. I had
ideas I wanted to express in script form which didn't fit the needs of
the employers. And I'd always done such a variety of things and this
was restricting me to TV shows.

They wanted to renew the contract for another year. I had this
strong intuitive feeling that if I kept going doing the same thing, the
signal to stop would come in the form of an illness. Something was
brewing because of the stress of overriding what I knew to be right
deep down, which was finding and following that path of creative
freedom, following my own direction not theirs.

The part of me which wanted to renew the contract spoke to me
about logic and money. The part that wanted to stop the whole thing
was arguing from creative freedom. It felt like such a relief to move
from the logic and money argument to the freedom argument. And
that was the deciding factor in the end. So I told them I wasn't going
to renew the contract, and then basically went back to a more
balanced way of working.

It was a moment that brought me back closer to the centre of what I am really about, rather than being caught up with other people's plans, with things that maybe I wanted at one point but had outgrown and which weren't important any more.

Similarly, Bart, a Dutch obstetrician, stopped himself before actually burning out, by saying a Great No and taking a leap of faith.

After a major reorganization which took away the sense of community in my hospital, the manager called me in and told me I wasn't scoring high enough on 'productivity' because I wasn't doing enough hysterectomies and caesareans. I took leave, went for a long ride on my bicycle, realizing how different a universe he and I lived in, and I came back and quit.

Bart's first move was to work with the dying. Recently, when I wrote to him saying I would like to quote him as an example of the Great No, he responded:

Last October I resigned from the hospice work. I had to create time. I have been occupied for the past year with founding a Cancer Help Centre in Rotterdam and also working as an obstetrician/gynaecologist on a part-time basis. I'm enjoying it very much. I'm doing well and I'm happy, never regretting the step I took three years ago saying the BIG NO!

These are all examples of people leaving their work or relationship. It can be just as life-changing to say a Yes and recommit to our old life. John, an entrepreneur, and Arnold, a doctor, both dealt with problems in their marriage by workaholism and by pursuing casual affairs. They started having classic burnout symptoms. Both, for different reasons, decided to recommit to their marriages, experienced relief and a new level of inner peace, and soon embarked on a very creative period in their lives.

Saying small yes's and small no's

When we cannot or will not say a Great Yes or a Great No, we may back down but pretend to ourselves that we aren't. We say small yes's and no's rather than a Great Yes or a Great No.

We can say a small yes to demands, a yes combined with resentment or resignation: *Yes, I'll help you, you bastard*. Or a small no to our truth, with rage and stubbornness: *No, I won't take that holiday I need, but I won't forget what you've done to me*. There is the quality of the victim in these yes's and no's. We may manage to say a small yes or no that is in the right direction: a small yes to our truth – *I will take a break as soon as I have a moment* – or a small no to inappropriate demands – *No, I won't do that for you today, but I will get it done*. But we don't admit that we have still decided to go on with what isn't true and healthy.

How can we tell a small yes or no from a Great Yes or a Great No? We can tell by how we feel. While the Great Yes and the Great No release our energy and creativity, the small yes's and no's swallow them up. While the Great Yes and the Great No leave us feeling expanded, a small yes or no leaves us contracted and diminished.

We cannot stay vibrant and happy and at peace when we compromise our truth.

As we try to avoid facing the implications of our compromises, we endanger our health even more. We take sleeping pills to continue functioning at the job that is keeping us awake, work harder to dull the pain of knowing we don't want to be there, drink alcohol or watch television to distract, disconnect and comfort ourselves, and then use chronic resentment to justify our disconnection. The more we escape, the less contact we have with our real selves, with intimacy with others, and with what nourishes us.

Not everyone who makes unhealthy choices burns out: some manage a stable though compromised life-style. Because they are able to do so, they may never consciously have to face the betrayal of their own selfhood. If we do burn out, this forces us to confront the areas in which we find it most difficult to face the truth. Our inability to tolerate lack of truth ultimately helps us to honour ourselves.

Why didn't we say a Great Yes or a Great No?

If we burnt out, we clearly did not say the Great Yes or the Great No that would have protected our health. Was it because the circumstances really didn't allow us to? Was it because we were too responsible or cared too much? Or were we just not willing or able to live truthfully?

It was not necessity that ruled

After burnout, all of us had to stop what we were doing in some way or other, some more drastically than others – some for a while and some permanently. While the losses were sometimes great, we all felt that we gained more than we lost.

If the world didn't fall apart and we actually benefited through the illness, it must be the case that it was possible to change something while we were still healthy. It could not have been pure necessity that ruled our actions. This was almost always clear to us in retrospect.

This doesn't mean that we had to up and leave the moment we wanted to. Barbara, managing director, decided she had to go, but then gave her company the time she assessed that they needed. This did not damage her health further, because she had said her Great No and probably operated differently after she had done so. Later she felt she had done it in the best way for all concerned and would continue to do so.

> I told the Chairman I wanted to leave. They offered me all sorts, six months' paid holiday, an Executive Director type position. But I can't do anything half measure. It was all or nothing. I said I was going to leave at Christmas and they ignored it and didn't do anything to find anyone to replace me. So I said I'd stay till March which is the end of the season and that's it, and I did. Now it's all falling apart. It seemed that they did need me to make it work. I don't feel guilty. I'm looking after the people I care about, I'm making sure they can get jobs if the company folds. But that's who I am.

We didn't burn out because we cared too much

It was also not 'caring too much' that kept us from protecting ourselves. If love is really our motivating factor, and we are being true to ourselves, we will not burn out. But much of what passes under the name of love or responsibility actually hides an unconscious investment.

What is wrong is not that we love or care too much or are too responsible. It is that we abandon our true selves.

There is nothing wrong with giving or sacrifice, even sacrificing our lives for someone else, if this is what our love and our truth call for. What is never okay is to give up our sense of who we really are. **We are not giving of ourselves . . . we are giving ourselves away.**

When we don't feel loving but think we should, there is often something that we are not listening to. Cara, art teacher, talked of how she couldn't acknowledge her body's messages and protect herself from a man who was endangering her because she wasn't supposed to be selfish.

> *My stomach was telling me the truth. I could feel it. Although my head was kind and my heart was open, my stomach was saying, 'Don't let this person within ten feet of you.' I got pains in my womb like a knife when he came near. A very deep part of me was saying – this is bad for you, this will hurt you. But I told myself I was being selfish. You must always have an open heart and be spiritual and helpful.*

When we don't take care of our own welfare, we collude with any tendency others might have to treat us badly. In the long run, this is not good for them either.

The Hawaiian Kahuna belief system holds that: *What is in our highest best interest is in the highest best interest of everyone around.* Allowing people to act unfairly to us, or to hang on to us when this is not good for us, or in any way to support what is not in our highest best interest, cannot in the long run be in their highest best interest either.

Under the guise of giving, we can also act in ways that are disrespectful and controlling of the partner or boss or child or parent we are doing this for. We expect them to receive our golden eggs, make use of them in the way we think is right, say thank you and care for us in return. When things don't work out as we hope, we can feel like victims and bitterly attack the other for betraying our expectations.

When we do stand up for truth, often what happens is that we create more and more honesty and real love all around us. I have watched whole family systems change when one person says what is true for them or acts in line with their truth.

At our growing edge

Neither necessity nor love stopped us from telling the truth. It was an unwillingness or an inability to honour our true self. Cut off from our own bodies and emotions, ready to give all to another without noticing our own needs, yet tied up with unconscious pictures of ourselves or dependencies on others, our ability to live truthfully is always at risk.

This doesn't mean that we are less truthful than other people or less honest than we 'should be'. It is not a moral judgment. It is simply that we were faced with a challenge to go beyond our old limits and we didn't quite make it. We were at our growing edge.

We are okay as long as the pictures we have seem more or less consonant with the reality. This is why a new job or a new relationship is often so blessed with the feeling of a dream come true. It is when the reality begins to diverge from our pictures, and we choose the pictures rather than the reality, that we can sink knee-deep in the mud of illusion.

Something was more important than the truth

Why do we choose our pictures over reality? We fear that if we face the truth, we will have to give up something we are deeply invested in, or do something that feels unfamiliar and threatening, or be seen by others as stupid or wrong or unacceptable. As in the case of Alice, something feels more important than the truth. This process is not always conscious, and sometimes it is accompanied by a terror so powerful that it feels almost impossible to do anything but succumb to it.

Leila, retreat director, talked movingly of the fear of speaking her truth.

Deep down it was a fear of annihilation. I could die if I spoke my real truth. Might be a child thing from my family: I would have been humiliated or an outcast if I was truthful. When you hit that block, you go to a place where there is no sound and no words.

Doris, accountant, was ignoring her health to keep her relationship alive.

Subconsciously I was saying: You are getting emotionally drained; the needle is going into the red part of the gauge. But I wasn't aware of that. I thought if I could get (John) right I could get our relationship back and then he would give me what I wanted.

Phil, insurance broker, said:

I was the kind of person who did the right thing, which means what I felt other people expected of me, and the part of me which wanted something quieter and gentler I would criticize and be judgmental of and wouldn't listen to.

Mary, airline planner, who was struggling with both her work and her relationship, told me:

I was holding on to the idea that I must be able to do this job because it's the right industry, I have the right experience and knowledge, and it's where I've always seen my future. So it has to be right. I told myself it was the perfect job. But it was making me unhappy. Not just the job but the relationship side of things. It was kind of unreal. There I was thinking that I'd got a good marriage and a happy affair and I could go on with both. But it couldn't stay like that because neither was complete. Neither could fulfil me; each was only a half. I couldn't be honest with either my husband or my lover and that stopped me also from being honest with myself.

Why didn't she tell herself the truth?

I guess some of it is to do with not wanting to admit I'd been wrong all that time. I'd been telling everybody that I liked my job that my relationship was good. But also, I knew that if I stopped and thought, I would have to change a lot of things and I was afraid to do that.

Dana, policy analyst, chose to do a prestigious MBA which she hated and began to burn out as soon as she started the course. She admitted that on some level she knew that this wasn't the right move.

There were many moments, for the first time in my life, that I thought of quitting. This was not what I signed up for. But I guess because of the financial commitment I felt like I had to do it. I thought people would look at me as if I was a fool – a fool in the first instance for doing it, and in the second instance for walking away from it, after all the money I spent. I never actually found out whether I could get the money back or not. And there's no one really to say it to me – just my mother. But I was frightened people would make fun of me and say I couldn't cut it.

Dana's mother really was standing by, ready to imply, but never say, that she couldn't cut it. Dana had made a similar choice once before:

There was something five years ago where I wanted to give up a job to earn less money on a presidential campaign. I didn't because my mother was saying, 'How are you going to pay the bills? How are you going to do this and that?' And I look at the sacrifices I made

*this year, and I realise I realise I could have made them then, but I
didn't because I was worried about giving up those salaries.*

As Dana left my home at the end of our session together I
found myself saying, 'Please, listen to your soul and not to your
mother.'

The power of someone else's will

Dana's mother probably had quite a powerful will and in her presence, Dana believed her mother was right and she was wrong. It is
very easy for us to forget our own point of view when we are faced
with the compelling point of view of someone who is powerful for
personal or social reasons. When this happens, it is not that we won't
follow our truth, but we get confused about what it is. Might has
become right.

Standing up to a powerful will can be especially hard for those of
us who are better at understanding the point of view of others than
remembering our own. It is even harder if our childhood experiences made this a very frightening thing to do. We become more
susceptible to allowing ourselves to be abused when we either
can't, or don't dare, remember our own point of view and stand up
for it.

Even if we do manage to find our truth and defend it, people can
send back strong messages that tell us we are bad and wrong to do
what we are doing. Someone else's need for power or control or
personal advantage may masquerade as something that is good for us,
and we often do not feel able to confront this hypocrisy.

The power of someone's will may be to do with their personality, or
it may be to do with the power relations between employers and
employees, men and women, adults and children, the social illusion
and the individual truth. Learning to stay in touch with our truth and
stand up to the powerful will of people and institutions is one of the
ways we slowly but surely learn to live truthfully.

Whose illusions are we protecting?

Our inability to say a Great Yes or a Great No is related to all our illusions about ourselves and about life, our outdated myths, and our ways of pleasing others or being acceptable. Maxine, a head-hunter when she burnt out and now a management coach, talked of the myths and illusions that had imprisoned her.

> I thought I could work seventeen hours a day seven days a week and still stand up at the end of it and smile and look glowing with health and a bundle of energy. I'd worked so hard at getting to where I was in 'society,' a successful businesswoman. I thought if I dropped it then the world would crumble somehow.

The illusions we are defending may not just be our own. We burnout people have a particularly bad record of protecting others at our own expense. Helen, artist, is suffering the effects of this protection racket.

Helen comes from a background of serious abuse by her stepfather with the collusion of her mother. Since she burnt out the first time, she has been working on becoming more honest, but she has still never spoken to her mother or stepfather about what happened, or dared in any way to shatter the old happy family myth that takes the upper hand whenever she sees them. While she is willing to dispense with her own illusions, Helen won't make waves with those of others. The repercussions of this unreality reaches into many areas of her life – how she acts, where she lives, what she can talk about, what she is free to do. Her secret contract to protect her mother and stepfather is so pervasive that it is possibly endangering her life.

Can we slow down enough to say yes or no?

When we are driving a car and come to a turning on the road, we know that we need to slow down in order to take the curve smoothly and safely. This is just what we don't do on the way to burnout. We don't take the time to figure out that we have a choice, and to consider what choice to make. If we did, we might find that the resolution to our problems is not out of reach, but simply a very big stretch away.

When I get people to go back to how they were at the time, to breathe and to watch that person, what they see is often remarkable. Barbara, managing director, described what she looked and felt like before she burnt out.

> *She's like a caged animal. A hamster running around a wheel. No way out. And not even able to run around the wheel as she would like to because her body won't let her. I get this vision of the phone ringing, and the deadlines for budgets, and deliveries, and all the different fifty million things of the day, even getting up out of the bath having to solve the problems of the day. Those problems never leaving you. Having to wake up with them. And always solving and discussing and planning. Who else is going to do it if she doesn't do it? And there are so many people relying on her. I have this vision of being on the phone and before I get off the phone, I have a list of people to phone back who were trying to get hold of me. There's definitely some sort of martyr stuff going on. I feel sick at the thought of it all. That I actually did it. It's that being trapped, no way out thing. The responsibility is just enormous. I don't know how I got out of it.*

In such an inner atmosphere, it is easy to see why inner truths or whispering bodies and souls were not listened to. When I asked Carol, health consultant, whether she could have listened to her truth and made a different decision when she was burning out, she told me:

> *I don't think so. What connects me most to my guidance is meditation or breath work or something that takes me inside. Everything was so blocked and tight that I lost touch with that without knowing I lost touch. There were so many demands on my time that I couldn't get to that still place I needed to be at.*

The irony is that what Carol was speeding around doing was teaching other people how to listen to themselves.

Not all of us speed up. Gwen, geophysicist, talked of her tendency to slow down and become unfocused, slapdash and haphazard when she begins to burn out. But this is not the kind of slowing down that promotes connection with oneself – quite the opposite. She described it this way: *'There's no longer a coherence. There's no nourishment from my core to support how I am living and what I am doing. Something is disconnected.'*

If we don't take the time, or don't have the habit of listening to what our soul is telling us about our own welfare, it is hard for us to make new and healthful choices. Yet those of us who are able to listen to relatively early symptoms and to reconnect to ourselves do not have to go through a full-blown burnout. It is a case of take time now or take a lot more time later.

Try This: Mind, heart and soul and/or Listening to my body

How can we know our truth? One way is to ask, as I have been asking you in exercises: *If my soul were whispering, what would it be saying?* Or try: *If I dared to admit what I really wanted, what would it be? If I could wave a magic wand over this situation, how would it be?* The following exercises can also work wonders.

Mind, heart and soul
This exercise of speaking from your control mind, your heart and your soul is a good stand-by at any time when you just don't know what's what. Remember that the control mind is the part of us that needs to keep everything secure and as it 'should' be and is in favour of caution, keeping to the old ways, not taking a leap. Our heart tends to speak up for love, for hope, for tenderness, for passion. Our soul tends to give a more varied answer and in my experience is usually closest to what is our highest and best truth, taking account not only of what we want and yearn for but also the reality of our situation and the wants and needs of others.

- Touch your forehead and say, 'What does my control mind say?' Whisper the first words that come to mind.
- Now touch your heart, and say, 'What does my heart mind say?' Again, whisper the first thoughts that come to you.
- Now imagine there is a light behind you that is larger than your body, and focus on that part of you. Now ask: 'And what does my soul say?' Again, whisper the answer.
- Reflect.

In a recent workshop of mine on *Love, Fear and Transformation*, Hannah was facing the question of whether she should quit her job. She worked with sick babies and was very good at it, but it was no longer good for her, and at the time she was off work with a serious back problem. She knew she was beginning to burn out, but both the fear of financial insecurity and the sense of her indispensability weighted heavily against her desire to leave.

As we explored the issue, I touched first her forehead, then her heart, and then signalled to the space behind her, asking her what her control mind, her heart mind and her soul thought. The response was swift.

Her control mind told her to stay because it was safer; her heart mind said, 'Give three months notice', and her soul said, 'Six months.' Six months turned out to give her the right amount of time for both her work-place and herself to make a smooth transition into a new future.

Listening to my body
Our body is a very reliable guide to our emotions and our truth. It can speak to us very graphically in images that illuminate what is going on not only psychologically but sometimes even physically.

- Focus on your body, and notice the first body part that comes to mind.
- Ask for an image to emerge of that body part or body feeling. Take the first image that comes to mind and allow

yourself to get to know it, have a conversation with it, ask it what it is telling you.

- Try 'becoming' that image by saying, 'I am this image' and breathing into the feeling of being that image. Speaking as the image, say what you are feeling and needing or what step you need to take so that you will feel better.
- Come back to being your human self and reflect.
- When you are ready, release that image from your body in any way that feels right. Then ask for an image that you would like to have there instead. When one comes up, put it in your body in place of the other one. How does this feel? What does this image want to say?
- During the course of the day, consider every now and then: With this new image in my body, how do I feel/what do I want/what is important?

Finally: Uncompromising truthfulness

The way forward doesn't always appear by magic when we stop and ask for it. It may not become clear for a long time. Yet just the trust that there is a way forward can get us to slow down, surrender, reconnect with our heart and soul, listen, watch, stay honest and wait until clarity emerges. This is enough. We won't stay confused forever.

The following words from the ancient book of Chinese wisdom, the *I Ching*, or Book of Changes, are related to the 'hexagram' or life situation called *Waiting (Nourishment)*. They are a perfect summing up of the Great Yes and the Great No.

One is faced with a danger that has to be overcome. Weakness and impatience can do nothing. Only a strong man can stand up to his fate for his inner security enables him to endure to the end. This strength shows itself in uncompromising truthfulness (with himself). It is only when we have the courage to face things exactly as they are, without any sort of self-deception or illusion, that a light will develop out of events by which the path to success may be recognized. This recognition must be followed by resolute and persevering action. For only the man who goes to meet his fate resolutely is equipped to deal with it adequately. Then he will be able to cross the great water – that is, he will be capable of making the necessary decision and of surmounting the danger. (p. 25)[1]

9

Burnout and Beyond
Choosing Radical Healing

There's an old saying that 'Experience is a hard teacher because she gives the test first, the lesson afterwards.'[1] Burnout is sometimes an even harder teacher. We may need to fail the test – or quite a few tests – before we get the lesson.

Sue Townsend felt that way about her repeated burnout:

I almost see myself as a seasonal thing. I burn out, I renew, I burn out, I renew. Each time I renew I get stronger rather than weaker, and happier, and more honest. And more able to include myself and what I want in thinking about other people's happiness.

While it is best if we stop ourselves before we burn out, we are not always able or willing to do so. This chapter takes us to that moment of burnout, to help us understand what it might feel like from the inside, and to see what our choices are then. Burnout, however it comes, and however many times it comes, often feels like the end of the road. Actually, it's only a crossroads.

Will we work to get our old show back on the road, or take the leap of faith involved in learning to listen to our soul and moving towards truly Radical Healing? If we choose Radical Healing, we need to be willing to step out of the world of clock and calendar time, to embrace that which we have been most afraid of, and to dip into the world of our imagination to hear the language of our soul. As we do so, we start on our new road to a radical reawakening.

Burnout

We have now traced the process whereby we move from whole-heartedness to burnout. We faced a change in which the heart went out of our situation, yet we continued onwards, driven by fear, ignoring warning signals and shutting off from the truth. As our soul withdrew its support, and we cut off from everything but our driven path, we moved from the inexhaustible energy of the universe to the limited energy of our personality.

Our investments were like magnets holding us in a negative situation. Our neglect of our welfare, and our dishonesty with ourselves and with others, allowed us to deny the implications of what was happening to us. Finally, we could ignore it no longer. Burnout.

What does burnout feel like?

Here are a few of the answers I got when I asked people what burnout felt like:

Exhaustion. I was driving myself to carry on and to work harder and harder and I was having to work harder to achieve the same or less. There were huge amounts of effort put into not achieving much, but I was pushing myself very hard. I felt exhausted and just couldn't carry on. I was disconnected from people. I started suffering from quite bad insomnia. I wasn't sleeping more than two or three hours a night. I finally realized it when I was chairing a meeting and everything that came up felt like a personal attack and I wasn't able to take the middle view. I felt responsible for things that had nothing to do with me. My boss sent me home that day because he felt that I wasn't coping and that I needed to do something to help myself.

Mary, airline planner

One day my back 'went out', and I literally 'backed out' of teaching school. I felt my world had come to an end, I had no more dreams, I felt old before my time, I was depressed, and had terrible back pain for eight weeks. A chiropractor came to visit at the house three times a week, as I could not get out of bed. Margaret, teacher

Suddenly I couldn't do a lot of the things I could do before – like driving into the city, or even going out socially. Apart from yoga and going for walks, I didn't do anything for six to nine months. I had pain, lots of pain, in my chest. Extreme tiredness, sleeping and sleeping and sleeping and I still felt tired. And tears, shuddering tears but also a different sort of tears. Even in the yoga class in the meditations on the heart, tears would flow like a river, just quiet like a river. That was so strange. I'd led such a busy life always, and if ever I'd been ill, two days or three days off was like an eternity. So when I went into this phase and it was two weeks – already something was amiss with the world. And then two months – I remember those time markers, thinking, 'This is not possible.'
Kelly, social worker

I was just fed up with living. That was the main symptom. Everything in life was an effort. There was no joy in anything I was doing. I couldn't feel anything and I wondered if I had any feelings at all. I think I'd been pretty shut down for quite a lot of my life but I was just absolutely emotionally dead. I felt like I'd lost all sense of who I was and what I was.
Edward, engineer

I went into a kind of blank space, where I was almost frozen into inaction and beyond caring what happened. Some days it was a heavy feeling, like wading through treacle and everything being an enormous effort, or like having your foot on the accelerator and the brake at the same time so that the net response was zero. Other days it just felt remote and disconnected and empty/indifferent.

I still more or less functioned day to day, in a going-through-the-motions kind of way, but the cracks began to show in other silly but completely uncharacteristic ways: things like going out and forgetting to turn the iron off, or realizing only at the very end of a day that I'd put on the jacket of one suit with the skirt of another that didn't go at all, and on a couple of occasions I lost my temper with different bosses. I knew I couldn't go on like this, but couldn't see an alternative.

I did carry on, at least in the week, but would long for the time when I could switch off and do nothing. I could hardly be bothered to

149

take my coat off or answer the door or the phone when I got in from work, and at weekends I'd often close the door on Friday evening and just slump until Monday morning. Sometimes I'd listen to friends leaving a message or an invitation on the answer machine but just not be able to face answering them. I felt mean and guilty about that, and I knew it wasn't the answer, but it felt like I was so close to the edge anyway that I'd just crack up if I started trying to pretend things were normal at home.   Carina, consultant

They had been like that burning bush that burns and doesn't consume itself. When they burnt out, they felt more like dust and ashes.

Is this the end of the road?

The beautiful thing about the human condition is that what looks like the end of a road never is. It is only the end of the road we know.

This is very frightening at first because it means stopping doing what is familiar and has gained us rewards in the past. We live in a culture in which stopping often signifies a failure to make the grade, to continue up the ladder, to win the prizes that are hanging at the top, or at least on the rung above us. As long as we are climbing, we are holding on to old identities or old beliefs about what we should be, and winning for ourselves the right to have new and more sparkling identities. If we lose these, who and what will we be?

Yet once we get to burnout, we often have no choice but to stop. Stop is of course what we need to do most of all. We need to stop fighting the burnout, indeed stop any kind of struggle. It is time for a new beginning.

But positive evolution doesn't happen by itself: we have to co-operate with it. We have a choice right now. Do we just want to get better and back on our old road? Or do we want to consider what brought us here, and find a new road altogether?

The first is familiar, seemingly safe, and is the way we know well. It does mean that we won't have learnt much and may end up at burnout point again. The second road goes toward Radical Healing and transformation, and towards cooperating with our own evolution. Obviously, I recommend Radical Healing. It is the real gift of burnout.

Radical healing

The Radical Healing approach is a totally natural one. People who have burnt out or even those who have early symptoms of burnout, often do this intuitively. I learnt this by doing it myself, and by feeling guided in that process by my soul, and so did many of the burnout people I know.

I call it Radical Healing because it is not about fitting back in, or even getting back our old wholeheartedness. It is about making that radical shift in the very basis of our lives that I believe that burnout is asking us to do. It is moving forward to a wholeness which involves all of us rather than just our wholeheartedness *about* something or someone else. It is also about opening a space in which joy dances, the space of just being ourselves and enjoying whatever life offers.

- Before, we loved and contributed in a way that was disconnected from important aspects of who we really are. Now, we need to reconnect.
- Before, we thought our contribution gave us value. Now, we need to see that it is we ourselves who are of value.
- Before, we thought we had to save the world singlehandly. Now, we can be part of an evolving creative whole.
- Before, our doing led to our being who we thought we were. Now, our being what we really are is what will lead to our doing.
- Before, we were wholehearted. Now, we are moving toward wholeness and joy.

Even if we are already following this path naturally, it helps to have a map that honours our path of transformation from wholeheartedness to burnout and then from burnout to joy. Too many of the maps around us and within us tell us we have an illness that needs curing, and we are doing something wrong if we are not getting better fast enough. As Jeff, counselling manager, said to me:

It has been very difficult to talk about my burnout because of all that Westernized cure-related, efficiency-based medical idea. I've reached out for help on all levels – psychiatrists, doctors, all manners of healers, and all have had a good effect but they haven't hit the mark in terms of me embracing what happened to me on that deep level. When you talk about burnout in this way, I can feel the relaxing effect it has on my heart, my body, my soul. Like I feel seen. You're not trying to drag me out of it.

Radical Healing is based on these steps:

- Wait. Give up hope. Keep the faith.
- Give your soul a good home.
- Build up your 'living truthfully muscle'.
- Open up to a soul community.
- When the way opens, don't leave your joy behind.

Each step opens more space for joy. Step by step we are led towards our new life.

The principle of paradox

Whatever it was that most threatened us, the shadow of our old life, turns out to be the light that will guide the way into our new one. Paradox is a basic principle of Radical Healing.

- *From hopelessness to giving up hope:* When we are burning out or burnt out, we probably feel pretty hopeless. Now we need to choose to give up hope. We will not get what we thought we wanted. Good. Now we can reconnect to ourselves and find out what is real right now.
- *From humiliation to humility:* We are probably feeling humiliated by the fact that we are not invincible, and we couldn't make the world the way we wanted it to be or believed it should be. We may be feeling like less than nothing – powerless even to get out of bed. Now we need to choose to give up

that wounded pride and find humility. Yes, we are limited and human. Good. Even the 'burnt-out case' we feel ourselves to be is of supreme value.

- *From disillusionment to de-illusionment:* We are probably deeply disillusioned by life or by our own reactions to life. What we believed didn't turn out to be true. Good. There must have been some illusion involved. It is time to 'de-illusion',[2] to let go of the illusions and go for what is true.
- *From the burnout of what we know to the light of what we don't yet know:* We are probably desperately mourning the fact that the world we have known and worked for is burnt out. Good. Now we can ask for our soul fire to light our way forward into what we do not yet know consciously but which is calling us.

Of course, the concept of the 'joy of burnout' is already a paradox. Burnout which seems to be a state of joylessness is actually pointing the way to joy.

Jeff talked in this paradoxical way about burnout as the recovery from what needed healing in his life.

The burnout is the recovery. It's like a friend who's actually been on your side through it all – totally on your side, truly on your side – and out of love takes you so that you literally lie flat on your back. It's trying to rest you into yourself, put you into your centre and into who you really are, and drench you in love.

Out of time is where we need to be

A central paradox in Radical Healing has to do with our attitude to time. Any book of wisdom we pick up will remind us to live in the present. For burnout people, coming back into the present is a matter of life or death. We need all our energy here in order to heal and to become whole.

When we were burning out, we were often running around trying to do the impossible to avert the unavoidable. We were terrified that we would run out of time.

In fact, out of time is where we need to be.

The centre of the paradox about time is to do with how, as in the hare and the tortoise story, the fastest parts of us are the furthest behind, while the slowest parts are way ahead, beckoning us.

While we are moving onward and upward in the world of calendars and clocks, our bodies, emotions, hearts, intuition and soul are moving much more slowly in their own very different dimensions. When we run, it looks as if we have left them behind. In fact the opposite is true. They leave us behind. In order to catch up with them, we need to slow down and stop. This paradox makes sense once we understand that we are operating in more than one time frame at once.

- Bodies have natural rhythms which are more like the rhythms of trees and lions than the rhythms of corporate life.
- Emotions may be caught in a time warp and reacting to situations which happened many years ago.
- Our hearts and our minds, when they work together, are more likely to sing or beat out a rhythm than to give a presentation or fix an appointment.
- Our intuition and our connection to others emerge in an instant without reference to boundaries of time and space.
- Souls may evolve through eternal time, but in comparison to our everyday clock time, they are almost standing still.

Compared to these, 'we', our everyday selves, seem to be much more speedy, efficient and in control. And yet:

- The inner feeling of our body tells us about what is happening on other levels of our being.
- Our emotions tell us about our longing and warn us of danger.
- Our heart and mind working together engage our passionate understanding.
- Our intuition and connection to others are a miracle and enable miracles to happen.
- Our soul's evolution far surpasses that of our everyday personality and opens us up to what is beyond.

Each of these aspects of our being is a guide or a doorway to a dimension of reality that we dare not live without. Each is picking up clues which our conscious rational sense misses. Most will whisper to us rather than shout. Working in alignment with each other, they represent our true intelligence and love. When we are speeding around, with our minds shouting about what we have to do next, we will miss these portals and fail to hear these whispers. We will run right into danger again and again and not notice for far too long.

It is only when our time runs out on us, which happens when we have burnt out, that we may do what was always needed: stop and be silent and in touch with our inner awareness enough to hear the whispers and notice the portals. As we take the time actually to listen and to walk through, we remember who we are.

Remember or discover? I think it is both. Being in touch with our deepest self always has that combination of deep recognition as well as a wonderful smile of surprise. We recognize that we are home, and breathe a sigh of relief, yet home has never looked quite like this before.

Imagery: The language of the soul

The best way I know to learn to listen to these whisperings is by reaching into our imagination, which speaks the language of the soul and is the bridge between that which we know consciously and that which we are about to know. We have already begun to do exercises using imagery as we have explored the pathway to burnout. This use of imagery can now expand and accompany us through all the steps of Radical Healing.

The imagination is the part of us that maps out the plans of how we experience life, and translates this into instructions or blueprints for our emotional, mental and physical systems. The imagination is also the means by which we can reach out to a wisdom that is beyond our present conscious knowledge. Everything we do, think, feel and believe that has any power is expressed in an image deep inside us. Imagery is the key to the integrated functioning of our entire organism. It also tells us of our highest dreams of how we might be.

We can use our imagination to tap into the underlying images that have driven us forward to burnout, and to find new images that can teach us how to fuel our fires differently in future. Imagery is an inexhaustible toolbox for drawing on the vast resources of our inner world to help illuminate our living and loving, and our future doing and creating and contributing.

Expanding your use of imagery

Each of the following chapters gives an idea of how to use the imagination to help support the process of healing. It is also worth consulting my book *Life Choices, Life Changes* for a comprehensive overview of Imagework – the art of using images to guide you and heal you in your life. You can also be guided through the images by using the set of eight *Image Power – Inner Power* tapes.[3] Here are a few general tips to start you on your way:

- Remember to use all your senses and take your time whenever you start working with an image. It is also good to become the various beings you imagine even if they are not people – to be the tree or the lion or the stone or the House of Truth or the healer that comes up in an image. Try having a conversation by switching roles back and forth. If you 'become' an image, actually step into it and breathe as this new person or being. If you are having a conversation, change seats or places each time you speak from another point of view. If it is about walking, as in the exercise *The crossroads* under Try This . . . below, try physically walking. Of course, if you are doing this on the underground or in a café, which is where I do a lot of my imaging, you need to be a bit subtle about it all.
- Whenever you want to understand anything, ask for an image. As an image emerges, treat it like a story with a past, a present and a future. Experience it from all perspectives: walk around, see it from above and below. Then become it and find out all about your essential quality and what feels important to you and what is hard. Ask yourself what led up to this moment in the story. You can take an aerial view as a wise and loving being looking down on the scene. Then find your next step as the image being, or wonder how it would be if you had a

magic wand. Do also draw the image, or dance it, or write a poem about it.

- Another approach is to treat everything as if it were already an image with a message for you. Rather than think *about* anything, talk to it and listen to its response. Talk to your aching back, or to the pile of papers on your desk, or to the trees outside your window, or to the statue that calls your attention in a museum, or to the disapproving face which is coming up in your mind. Focus on it, allow yourself to surrender, ask anything you want to ask, and wait for an answer.

- Imagery has a capacity to go straight to the point. Don't be afraid of this. Just keep breathing and keep understanding. Your knowing will eventually lead you to a place of peace, not harm. Just living with the images will be healing, even without looking for answers and transformations.

- The methods we focus on during the Radical Healing period are mainly not images of the future, but images of the present and past. This is because the first step after burnout is always to stay with what is. Only when you are ready, and the energy is freely flowing, is it safe to start to have images of the future.

- Images are everywhere, and can be expressed in various ways. Poetry, art, movement and voice are all ways to express our imagination. Myths and dreams speak the language of the imagination. This means that by steeping ourselves in all these forms of creativity, whether as consumers or creators, we are giving parts of ourselves a voice that they have never had.

One of the most beautiful things about using imagery when we've burnt out is the discovery that what felt like an empty house burning on the outside and charred on the inside, is actually a palace full of treasures we have never taken the time to discover. This is the palace of the soul.

The choice we always had

The choice we face when we are completely burnt out is not new. Whether we are burning out, burnt out, or just wondering whether burnout lies this way, what we have to do is the same. We need to listen to our truth and choose a way forward that will get us and keep us healthy and reconnected to ourselves and to life.

The earlier we do it, the more effectively we can take responsibility for our health instead of waiting till our health takes responsibility for us by shutting down. I myself left it a bit late – only two or three weeks too late – but it was many years before I recovered. When our physical or emotional or mental resilience is threatened, we cannot predict how far-reaching the result will be. It is no longer in our hands.

If you haven't yet burnt out completely but can see the signs, you have time to work your way quickly through the steps of Radical Healing. Once you have burnt out completely, you have the advantage of having enough time to go through the kind of slow transformation that changes you from the inside out. But you probably also have to heal the secondary effects of whatever physical, emotional or mental symptoms have incapacitated you. I'm writing on your prescription pad: Radical Healing, A.S.A.P.

Try this: Your burnout story and image, and the crossroads

Your burnout story and image

- Write down everything that makes you think that burnout has something to do with you. Try writing it like a story in the third person. Or write it as a letter to someone, real or imaginary, who understands you and loves you; or as a letter *from* someone who loves and understands you and wants to tell you what they have been noticing. Or just start off writing, 'Dear me, I wanted to tell you about me and burnout' and see what you write next.

- Include any changes in your life, choice points you've faced, investments you may have feared losing, ways you've neglected your welfare, areas in which you've been dishonest with yourself. List any possible symptoms of burnout, including those that may not be anything to do

---

with burnout but happened suspiciously around a time of stress, conflict or disillusionment.

- Sit quietly, perhaps with your eyes closed, and just ask for an image to emerge of an animal, a plant or an object that represents your burnout. Whatever comes up, look at it from all sides, from above, and from underneath. Then 'become' the image, breathing into being it. How do you feel physically, mentally, emotionally, spiritually as this image being? What is happening for you? What led up to your present situation? What do you really want?
- Now take some colours and, while meditating on your image, start making marks. Don't try to make a picture unless one emerges. Just choose the colours that feel right and let your fingers do the talking. When you finish, put some words on the picture.
- Reflect on what has emerged for you and how you feel about it.

The crossroads
- Imagine that you are standing at a crossroads. If you can, actually stand up and do the rest of this exercise on your feet, walking. Otherwise, imagine it with sound, colour, texture, smells. Put the story and the picture next to you as your voice of truth. Reflect on what has brought you here.
- Ahead of you are two paths. One says, 'The way I know: getting the old show back on the road' and the other says, 'The way I don't yet know: towards Radical Healing'.
- Start walking on the one that feels most attractive. What can you see, feel, experience? How are you walking – skipping, trudging, or what? Whisper out loud as you walk, saying whatever comes to mind.
- At some point stop and say, 'Now it is five years later on this path. What is happening now?' Keep whispering out loud.
- Turn and look back at the crossroads where you were

standing. If you could say something to that person who was standing there, what would you say?

- Now go back to the crossroads, and try the other path and do the same.
- Float above and take an aerial view. You may find some surprises.
- Then come back to the crossroads. Rename the paths with names or symbols that express your own experience of them.
- Which one will you choose? Take the first three steps on that path, very slowly, and as you take each step see if you can get a sense of what that step is. Let any word or image come to mind as you take that step.
- Reflect on what all this has meant to you.

Finally: Do read on

Whichever path you have chosen, do read on and find out more about Radical Healing. If you have chosen the way you don't know, this is your road map. If you have opted for the way you know, you will find some tips to help you manage it better. And as you get used to the idea, you might come back to the crossroads and choose Radical Healing next time. In any case, starting a healing diary, a few ideas for which follow this chapter, is a good first step.

And whatever you choose, make sure it is a Great Yes or a Great No. That way lies joy.

Your Healing Diary

This is a good time to start a diary that tells the story of your healing. Get yourself a notebook or file that attracts you. Then follow this one rule: Record one thing each day that you feel is a step towards your healing and transformation.

It could be a walk, a meditation, a swim, an exercise class, an insight, a Try This . . . exercise from this book, an honest confrontation, a decision to wait rather than rush into something, an openness with a new soul friend, or whatever. Make sure it is something that is consciously a contribution towards your healing rather than something you would do anyway. You might want to think about:

- What happened?
- What did you learn?
- What surprised you?
- What didn't?

Or you might write a poem, do a picture or a collage, write a letter to yourself, or whatever represents your experience of feelings best for you.

It doesn't have to be something that 'got you anywhere'. You showed up.

Radical Healing:
From Burnout to Joy

10

No way Forward but to Stop
Wait

A few years ago, when I took a four-month trip around the world, I made a point of becoming more at home with the great rocks and trees who move so much slower than I do. As I tried to talk with them and listen to their point of view, I developed a little mantra: *Wait. Give up Hope. Keep the Faith.* When I returned, I told my friend Hazel about this phrase, and she immediately started quoting these lines from T. S. Eliot's poem *East Coker*,[1] which I hadn't read since college.

> *I said to my soul, be still, and wait without hope*
> *For hope would be hope for the wrong thing; wait without love*
> *For love would be love of the wrong thing; there is yet faith*
> *But the faith and the love and the hope are all in the waiting.*
> *Wait without thought, for you are not ready for thought:*
> *So the darkness shall be the light, and the stillness the dancing.*
> (pp. 200–201)

Waiting without hope, for hope would be hope for the wrong thing, is the first step, and one of the greatest joys, of healing from burnout. Indeed, the whole of the poem *East Coker* could be called a map of the burnout journey.

The simple programme that can guide us in our first fumbling steps towards joy is expressed in these words:

Wait. Give up hope. Keep the Faith.

This chapter is about that first step: Wait. And while we wait, we breathe and we listen.

Burnout has to do with our unwillingness to surrender – to our bodies, hearts and souls and to reality itself. Healing begins at the moment we do surrender. We have to admit that we don't know where we are going, so we need to stop going anywhere. As we wait, we listen to all the voices we have ignored and eventually find a place in us that can withstand the waves of feelings and yet be at peace. We begin to discover, also, that we need not feel trapped by circumstances again.

Wait

When I mention waiting, you may groan and want to say, as so many have:

> *Does this mean I must leave my job or my relationship? What if I can't afford to? Do I give up my responsibilities? What about all the people who will suffer? Isn't that a pretty selfish thing to do? And dangerous?*

What waiting doesn't mean
Doubts and fears often arise because we have two contradictory pictures of what stopping and waiting would mean, both extreme. We have catastrophic fantasies of everything falling apart if we stop, and wonderful fantasies of giving everything up. We are probably speeding up faster and faster precisely because we don't want to face the fact that we'd rather give it all up.

Yet waiting doesn't mean making a decision to leave, or to stay, or to do anything at all about our future. We have no idea what is right for us because we are so out of touch. That is why we are waiting.

What waiting does mean
Waiting means that we have to stop trying to accomplish whatever it is that we are trying to accomplish, and averting whatever catastrophe we are trying to avert.

We have to give up the struggle.

This is not a withdrawal into deadness, but rather an active process, a kind of heightened awareness. We stop, breathe, let go of what we are holding on to, and wait – for the well to fill with water from the underground spring, for the tree to flower again after months of drought, for the bird to heal its wing so it can fly.

We give ourselves time and space to enable this to happen, but don't make any decisions beyond this. Stopping is the decision, and there is no way to predict what further decisions will emerge. Whatever emerges, we will only act if we want to.

Taking a break

It is a good idea, if at all possible, to take a break by being somewhere other than the centre of the action. Whether we choose to sit or mountain-climb or dance, what is important is the quality of stillness at the heart of it.

Sometimes this stillness brings its own wisdom. Gwen, geophysicist, talked to me about how she walked her way to quitting her job.

The Sierra Club were doing the Colorado trail, and I signed up for two weeks of it. I was sitting in this blues bar in Hoboken, New Jersey and I asked myself: 'Give me one reason why I shouldn't do the whole thing.' The whole thing was eight weeks which meant I would need to resign. I couldn't think of any reason not to do the whole 500 miles, so I quit my job.

Leila, retreat director, went to her niece's wedding held in the mountains:

I was given this room on my own, and suddenly there was all this space. I was on top of a mountain and I could see for miles. I was meditating in this window and I could hear the inner voice so clearly. It wasn't possible not to respond.

That inner voice was telling her to take leave from work. When she did, she again found it helpful to go to a new environment.

I took myself to Canada for five months. I met people, and I opened myself more to what my body is about. I could also express myself more freely and just unlock my system and sense who I was at a different level – discover a different way of being me. And I could find out what energizes me and what drains me. It was so much easier because I was away from the vortex of my life.

Who has time for that?

Taking some kind of break often seems impossible. Perhaps it is. But don't forget: nothing is served by letting our bodies stop us instead of stopping ourselves, except, in the short term, our pride.

The Sabbath principle

If you really and truly cannot take a break, you can still stop and wait. This takes more discipline but it can be done. Operate day by day to do what is essential for life that day. Give up achieving or going forward. You are not going anywhere now.

A Jewish tradition that I love is the Sabbath – Friday night and Saturday – when there is an underlying rule that we don't do what is necessary for tomorrow, only that which is for today. When we are burning out, every day needs to be a kind of workday Sabbath. Sufficient unto the day is the work thereof.

Become as clear as you can about what is urgent, and then stop worrying. Do what calls you today. Tomorrow something else will call you. Our deepest being knows what's truly urgent and will let us know. The false alarms saying *Emergency, Emergency* take up more energy than we can afford right now.

Even if we are not taking a break, we need to have breaks in our day and a whole day a week which are our times for stillness and delight. Any form of meditation, or walking in nature, or making music or dancing, or visiting a peaceful place can help with the discipline of waiting. So can anything that makes our heart sing. How we do it is a personal choice. It is the decision to stop the struggle that is crucial.

Struggle is the tinnitus of our lives

Stopping the struggle may necessitate penetrating to the core of what is a constant background atmosphere of our lives. Many of us take struggle for granted as one of those uninvited permanent guests of our consciousness. It is a hum that doesn't go away, a tinnitus that we've stopped noticing because it is always there.

In my Imagework courses, we sometimes do exercises in which we imagine our births or our deaths. Although it is normal to think of birth as good and death as bad, people actually experience birth as a struggle and death as a relief.

There is something about the quality of relief which people feel when they cross over from life, the knowledge that the struggle is over, which we seem unable to allow ourselves while we are alive. I find *The bridge*, under Try This . . . below a lovely way to give us a sense of how it might be if we could.

They also serve who only stand and wait

You may feel guilty about stopping and waiting because you are not contributing. Yet the world is built on a balance of giving and receiving. You have given. That way has come to an end. Now it is time to receive. If you allow yourself to receive for long enough, a new shape of you will emerge, and a new form of giving.[2]

When I was a kid in my Jewish school, the Yeshiva, we used to have to collect money for charity. The usual response when I knocked on someone's door to ask for money was 'I gave already.' Try telling yourself *I gave already* next time you feel yourself reaching in your pockets for your last energy penny.

Waiting is breathing time

While we wait, we have time to appreciate our breathing. This understanding came through to me when I participated in a retreat with Vietnamese monk Thich Nhat Hanh,[3] or Thay. I went to his monastery in France at a crucial moment when I had given up everything I knew about the future and needed to learn how to live in the present.

Thay reminded us again and again to be happy because we breathe. Every fifteen minutes a gong would ring to remind us to stop and breathe. Each step we took had to be slow enough for us to stay conscious of our breathing. Waiting in queues for food – no problem –

breathing time. Our breath comes first and everything else second. Being alive is the point – not what we are doing and achieving.

Our breath is a blessing that comes to us not because we are special or privileged but because we are alive. Not only that, but our joy in our breath is also for others because we are all interconnected. Thay would say: 'When I breathe, I breathe for you. When I walk, I walk for you.' Our very living, if we slow it down and tune into our essentials, can be a way of connecting and rejoicing on behalf of all humanity.

As we left the retreat, I was irritated by the idea of a day of travelling that mostly consisted of waiting around wasting time. My friend Judith just said, 'Time for breathing.' Waiting is not wasted time any more. Time for breathing.

Listen, listen, listen

If we've burnt out, it is always the case that we have stopped listening to ourselves for long enough to 'lose the plot'. When we wait, we also have to stop denying and take up listening again. Listening is food for our hungry soul.

What we do to avoid pain causes pain

Listening to ourselves means finding our real shape and form. It also means hearing all the contrary voices inside us that tell us to be a different shape. Then there are the fear and rage reactions to these voices; then level after level of our hopes, dreams, fantasies and illusions; then the loneliness and hopelessness and powerlessness and fears that make up the abyss that we have defended against. Beyond all this, there is deep peace.

What we do to avoid pain causes pain.

All the ways we have defended ourselves against pain, from tension to confusion to addiction to drivenness to critical voices are now themselves causing us pain. This is the first layer we will experience. Everything we have been shutting down will also come up. They are all coming up to be healed. But it won't feel that way.

It may be good to have a counsellor or psychotherapist or coach to help you through this transitional period: many burnout people feel they couldn't have got through as successfully without this. Others did it on their own or with friends and family. Do at least talk with someone you trust about how it is for you now. Allow yourself to think out loud in their presence. This is far more powerful than just thinking inside our heads.

Some listening principles

If I want to listen to you in a compassionate and helpful way, I naturally follow these principles:

- I love and respect you and know you are going to be okay.
- I encourage you first to stay with your feelings and then to make sense of them.
- I give you time and space to come to your own resolution.
- I help you explore new choices without criticizing what you did in the past.
- I honour a deeper level of who you are beyond all these feelings.

This is what we also need to do for ourselves:

I love and respect myself and know I'm going to be okay
When we wait and listen, we are not initially going to find out how wonderful we are. In fact, we are probably feeling pretty awful, and pretty bad about ourselves. The most important message we can give ourselves is something like this:

> *This is hard, really hard. I'm going to do it in the easiest and most loving way I know how. I'm going to take it slow, not expect too much, and trust that I'm going to be okay. I am already okay. It's just hard to feel it right now. I will feel it when I'm ready. Until then, I'll just do my best.*

I encourage myself first to stay with my feelings and then to make sense of them

Carina, consultant, told me about the extreme feelings she had after she burnt out and quit her job:

> There was a huge sense of release and excitement as I embarked on a number of little courses in creative things like writing and dancing – amongst them a holiday in Skyros. I felt guilty, half expecting someone to tap on my shoulder and demand to know what I was playing at, and why I'd not been in the office. I often felt empty and helpless, because I knew that really I had no idea what to do next, or how to go about finding out. One time I got a job interview lined up for myself, only to wake up on the day and immediately start crying uncontrollably – feeling utterly feeble and weak, and that I just couldn't go through with it.
>
> I felt upset when I thought it hadn't just been me, and I was sorry I'd been bullied into believing it was. Sometimes I'd lurch between extremes: blistering rage one minute, blubbering tears the next. It all felt out of control – I didn't feel like me, or know what me should feel like. I feared disintegrating completely – as if, in letting go and trying to relax, I was just dissolving into a helpless blob. I felt disappointed with myself that I was being so pathetic, but my rational and emotional selves seemed to be out of synch.

When all these feelings come up, it is easy to want to go up into our control minds and tell ourselves why we shouldn't be feeling this way. This only makes the feeling persist, like the complaints of a child who is told that he should grow up and stop being a nuisance. Instead, we need to go down to a stable, quiet part of ourselves and try to stay with the feelings until they reveal their truth.

There is nothing wrong with our emotions. They are the right response to what is sometimes the wrong perception.

No matter how crazy or extreme they seem, our feelings are real and need to be honoured. After we have done this, we can look at why we were reacting that way, what perceptions led to those reactions, and whether or not the perceptions were accurate.

There is usually some truth in our feelings which we need to find and acknowledge. Our anger might be telling us to say no and protect ourselves; our anxiety – that something has shaken us to the core; our shame – that someone has humiliated us.

Not all the feelings are our own. We may have absorbed other people's without being aware of it, particularly if we were in a situation where emotions were not out in the open.

Once we have understood our feelings, we can step back and ask ourselves: *If I had a bigger picture, or a bigger perspective, what would it be?* and wait to see what picture emerges. For example: *Yes, I am furious and frightened about leaving my job and in a larger sense it was time to go.* Notice that it is an *and*, not a *but*. Both are true, just on different levels.

I give myself time and space to come through to resolution
When we are in the midst of powerful feelings, it feels hard to believe they will ever end. Yet it does seem to be true that if we give ourselves the time and space, we do come to rest. Mary, airline planner, told me what happened when she first signed off work:

> *I didn't do anything. I still wasn't sleeping, and I just sat and existed for about two weeks, just feeling the feelings and admitting what was in there. It took a few weeks and bit by bit the sleep came back. I started to feel I had more energy, and found activities for myself and actually started to make plans instead of just thinking 'I've got to carry on.'*

Janey, health consultant and editor, saw the process as a detoxification from the years of work stress and of pushing down her feelings:

> *It wasn't like I skipped out of the office, threw my shoulder-pads and diary to the wind, and said 'Yippee.' There's been a lot of loneliness, a lot of uncertainty, a lot of depression, tears, feelings I had pushed down. And that sense of having no idea where my life is going.*
>
> *But I think also that you store in your body these stress hormones and there is this toxicity. I had twenty-five years of full-on full-time work without a break, getting hooked into all that stuff that you have to do to survive in a working life and perform no matter how*

you feel. And actually I liked being famous and earning all that money – it was a safety net. So it was hard to lose that.

It's all been a real struggle, like weaning myself from an addiction. It took a long time to detoxify. Detox is what it feels like. But I'm just beginning to feel that this is going to be all right.

I explore new choices without criticizing what I did in the past

Struggling with the fact that we burnt out, we can feel like helpless victims of a situation we were trapped in. It helps to go back and see what really happened and what options we had that we weren't aware of. The exercise *The defining moment* under Try this . . . below can help you do this.

Seeing a new choice now doesn't mean we should have done it then.

If we could have, we would have. It does mean we are not helpless or trapped when things go wrong. Next time we are at risk, we may be able to do things in a new way.

I honour a deeper level of who I am beyond all these feelings

Much of what we will be hearing inside us is the storm of our emotions. It is good to remind ourselves that we are like a sea whose turbulence on the surface doesn't tell us anything about the world that is going on in its depths.

This is why along with listening to our feelings, it is important to take the time to go deeper into a level which is quiet enough for us to hear the whisperings of the soul. Any form of meditation practice at the beginning and end of each day helps us to do this. The exercise *Breathing and expanding* under Try This . . . is also a good way to acknowledge the feelings and rest in what is beyond them.

Try This: The bridge, Breathing and expanding and The defining moment
The bridge
This image can help us move between the world of outer reality and struggle and the world of our aspirations or our

soul, which is without struggle. It can also help us to sleep when it is hard to let go of the day's struggles.

- Imagine that you are in a landscape which includes a river or a stream. Stamp your feet until you really feel the ground under your feet. See the colours, smell the smells, hear the sounds. Dip your feet in the water.
- A wooden bridge appears. Begin to walk on the bridge, feeling the wood under your feet, holding on to the wooden handrails, enjoying the old wood.
- As you walk on the bridge, it slowly begins to turn to light and you turn to light. When you reach the other side, you, the bridge and the landscape are all light. Somewhere in the middle the bridge has become light and so are you. Now explore that light world and see what happens and who you meet. Find the quality of being you that is different.
- When you have finished exploring, you may want to go back over the bridge to the real-world side. Notice what happens as you and the wood become real. See what you can bring back with you. Going back and forth over the bridge can be a meditation practice.
- If you're using this to fall asleep, you probably won't get back! Enjoy the light.

Breathing and expanding.
This form of breathing and listening is a synthesis of meditation and Imagework. It is a way of coming back to ourselves and listening to our feelings as well as to our deepest being. It can also be used when you feel troubled or unsure what to do.

If you are not used to meditation or imaging, start by giving yourself five or ten minutes of quiet time. Do more if that is comfortable. Once you get the hang of it, you can do a one-minute version even in the middle of the action.

Remember you are not trying to get anywhere. You are just stopping and expanding, like a sponge that is filling with water after lying dried out and neglected.

- Begin to notice your breathing. Just think, *I am breathing in. I am breathing out. Breathing In. Breathing Out. In. Out.* As you do so, notice all the feelings that come up. Smile at whatever feeling comes up, imagine wrapping it with light or love or a white cloud, and let it float off. Ask for it to be released from every cell of your body and to be replaced with a smile or with love. Go back to the breathing, and repeat this process a few times. Every feeling that comes up is fine, every thought is as it is meant to be. Just smile at them lovingly, let them go, and return to your breathing.
- Now imagine that you have an energy field around you or a circle of the radiance that comes from you. Breathe in and out a few times. Now imagine that that field or circle is expanding to twice its former size. Continue with the breathing and noticing thoughts and feelings as above.
- Keep expanding the energy field – let it be as big as the room, then your city, then the earth – until you feel whole and as big as you can be. With each expansion, do the breathing and notice the feelings. Take your time. Keep expanding. Keep breathing. Keep feeling. Keep on keeping on until you come to rest.
- Ask yourself now: *Who is he or she who has had all those feelings and thoughts?* Keep asking this question until you have a sense of a quiet essence of just being you. Go into the feeling of that essence of being you, he or she who experiences being you, and just stay with that presence for a while, breathing and enjoying the peace.
- At the end of this, notice how you feel and how the world looks. If there is something you are confused about, ask for some help and just wait and see whether an image or thought comes up to clarify things. Come to rest.

The defining moment
I suggest that sometime when you are feeling courageous, you use this exercise to go back in your imagination to the situation you were in before you burnt out.

- Find that defining moment or moments or period when your energy cycle stopped being positive and fulfilling, and became negative and draining. You may have looked at this moment if you did the exercise *What about you?* under Consider This . . . in Chapter 5.
- Picture the scene in full colour and texture as if you were standing outside it and looking in. What do you notice that the person in there doesn't know about themselves? Rise above as if you are a wise and loving being looking down on yourself. What do you notice now that they don't know about themselves?
- Now enter inside yourself and breathe until you feel yourself in the body of the person you were then. Feel the feelings and see the world as then.
- Now do the *Breathing and expanding* exercise until you come to rest.
- Allow yourself to notice what now seems possible or clear that wasn't before.
- You might want to go back outside to look at how you look from the outside or from above, to see if you seem different now.

Finally: Dwelling off the map

Waiting and just breathing and listening can feel like hell to those of us who think doing is the only way of being and who know only too well all the things that are waiting to be done. But waiting is also a great privilege. It reminds us that where we are at this very moment is itself a real and lasting place, and not just a way station to the future. Also, who we are at this moment is of great value, even when we have nothing to show for it but ourselves.

We may wonder who and what we are waiting for. Let us keep wondering. We are getting to know the space of not knowing. This is the only way through to a new kind of knowing and being. In T. S.

Eliot's words: 'In order to arrive at what you are not, you must go through the way in which you are not, and what you do not know is the only thing you know.'[4]

We are dwelling off our old map. This was once terrifying. As we embrace it willingly, it becomes a relief and a pleasure.

11

Neither Hope nor Hopelessness
Give up Hope, Keep the Faith

One sunny afternoon, I was working with a group in our Atsitsa centre in Skyros on resolving our unfinished business with important people in our lives. People were sitting around the stone circle we call the Magic Circle, overlooking the trees and the sea, conducting whispered conversations with various people in their lives, living or dead. There was a surrealistic flavour to the scene.

Suddenly one young man, Matt, began to sob in a heartrending way. He had just seen and acknowledged that his mother really didn't love him after all.

To everyone's surprise, yet not to Matt's, I said, 'Good, now you know.'

I sensed that the moment Matt acknowledged what seemed to be a hopeless loveless reality, he could give up on his life-long doomed efforts to gain his mother's love and open up to a new life full of the love that really was available to him now. Some day he might revisit this conversation with his mother, and realize that on another level, his mother did indeed love him, though not in the way he once needed and expected.

Without giving up his old hope for the love of his mother, Matt could not let go of his hopelessness and lovelessness and move towards love and joy. This is one of those paradoxes of Radical Healing.

We have now begun to wait and listen. This chapter is about how we can take a further step by giving up hope both for the future and for the past, while still keeping the faith. Although this may lead us through feelings of despair, resentment and regret, it will also bring us to the moment when we acknowledge what it is we can trust and surrender to. We are then free to be in the present. Before that, we were living in hope. Now, we can begin just to live. This is one of the most important lessons burnout has to offer us.

Give up hope for the future

We often say, 'Hope is the only thing that keeps me going.' Yet so often hope is what T. S. Eliot called 'hope for the wrong thing'. It is for something that we once believed we wanted but may no longer be right for us, if it ever was. What we really need is more like trust in an unfolding than a hope that a particular dream will come true. This trust has the sweetness that we usually attribute to hope, without the risk of illusion and disillusionment.

Hopelessness and giving up hope
When we are burning out, there is usually a combination of profound hopelessness and rigid hope. We are in despair of ever getting what we hoped for and yet we are striving, hope against hope, to get there anyway. We want what we want, and we'll die if we don't get it. So we nearly kill ourselves trying.

Jeff, counselling manager, talked movingly of everything he had to give up:

> I had to give up everything – my identity, my future, where I was going. I had to give up the identity of dynamic entrepreneur who got involved with these big projects and went on television. I had to give up the identity of being a psychotherapist. I had to give up my identity as being a certain kind of friend – sweet, very kind, but too kind, and someone who didn't rock the boat. I had to give up money. For the first time in my working life, I was poor, and still am. So I had to give up some of the other things – glamour – someone who wore certain kinds of expensive clothes, and went to some of the best restaurants and was one of the elite trendy. I had to give up being trendy and interesting. I had to give up being the son I'd been to my parents who didn't rock the

*boat and who compromised his life for them. I had to give up rescuing
my brother – he was mentally ill and I couldn't save him. I had to give
up control over what fate had dealt me and my family.*

Giving up hope is the opposite of hopelessness because it is trusting
in ourselves and in what we may be, given half a chance and loads of
patience. But when we stop and wait without hope, our first movement can sometimes be into depression and hopelessness. This form
of depression is how we mark the shedding and death of an old part of
ourselves, or of an old fantasy about ourselves.

When we give up on old dreams, we do need to grieve them. There
is no way around that. And most of us have to give up hope more than
once. No matter how bad it feels, remember that this is just nature's
way of mourning something that it is time to leave behind. Julie, arts
organization director, talked about how she felt depression was
necessary for her:

*I had to go right to the bottom, to accept that the mask had slipped.
There was no Holy Grail and no Golden Fleece. It's like waking up
on Christmas night, and realizing that there is no Father Christmas.
I allowed myself to despair, to be depressed, to taste the ashes. For a
while I couldn't see any hope in the future. I felt I was a complete
waste of oxygen and my life was utterly pointless. And I just allowed
myself to let go. It was a bit like I'd ripped up my life completely and
had to start again.*

If you do get depressed, please resist the temptation to attack
yourself and tell yourself that it is all your fault that you have ended
up here. You have not ended up here. You are letting go of what has
ended in order to open up to the new. This is also not a time to believe
you are alone in your own private hell. Reach out. Share. Give and
receive love. Challenge the humiliation. Discover trust. When we
don't blame or isolate ourselves, this low period passes more quickly
and can have a sweetness of healing about it.

This is not to say that you *will* get depressed. Many people don't.
But giving up hope can be tough and if it does lead you briefly into

despair, you can, so to speak, take me with you there. I know what it is like. I know how it feels in the depths of Never Never Land, when we are certain that we'll never never never have what we want. You definitely will, though you may be wanting something very different by then.

The relief of giving up hope

Giving up hope is not always painful. It can even be a joyful relief, particularly when we do it at those moments when we are keyed up with excitement and worry. Perhaps we have a plan which we believe is the only possible option in the world, but which we fear could go terribly and disastrously wrong. Or perhaps we have a problem we must resolve right now or else. But what if we can't? But we have to!

Wait. Give up hope. All that stressful package of feelings melts away. We breathe a great sigh of relief. We look around and within and notice the beauty of now.

When that happens, we can get a whiff of that joy that arises in the spaces and not in the crowded reality of our plans and promises. It kind of breathes 'Me, now, how wonderful.' Thich Nhat Hanh (Thay) calls it 'Present moment, wonderful moment'.

This is the best you've been able to imagine

Whatever picture you have of the future, just let the picture dissolve. Give up hope of it ever happening. Then breathe. You don't know what you don't know, and the reality may be far better than anything you are imagining now. As my friend Clare once told me, 'Reality is always so much more interesting than the fantasy.'

The trouble with our pictures of the future is that they are based on how we are right now, in our present shape. The shape we are now is not a free and flowing one with unlimited possibilities, as it may once have been. It is the result of how we've fitted in with our partner or our work or our parents or whomever or whatever has shaped us in our lives. As we held on tight during the run-up to burnout, that shape probably got even more rigid. Even if we have separated ourselves and now seem to be free, our shape is the same.

Perhaps we are the shape of someone who serves powerful people. If we try to imagine a different future, we may imagine finding someone powerful in a different way, or someone who will see us as powerful and serve us. But this is just a different version of the old story. Our shape hasn't changed. We've just moved a notch.

This is why it is so crucial to wait long enough for us to get back into our own original flowing shape before we begin to try to look into the future. Only then can we be free and open enough to find a future that fits who we really are, and who we might be becoming.

This future we have been holding on to is the best that we have been able to imagine. Time to let go of it. We will imagine better.

Give up hope for the past

On my study wall there is a bumper sticker given to me by Abagayle, a woman who works with murderers on Death Row after having come to forgive the man who murdered her daughter. It says:

Forgiveness is giving up all hope for a better past.

This is the other half of giving up hope – letting go of all our plans for the past.

But it's not fair

As we give up hope, what often emerges besides the sadness and mourning is regret and resentment. These are two sides of the same coin.

Regret says: 'If only I'd done it differently . . .' If only we had done it all differently, we could still have everything we had before. We are idiots or worse.

Resentment says: 'If only someone else had done it differently.' Someone else did not save us, indeed someone else had caused this problem for us by being inhumane, abusive or worse.

Either way, *It's not fair!* It shouldn't have been this way. This shouldn't have been allowed to happen. Whoever's at fault mustn't get away with this – we or they must learn. Otherwise it can happen again. This lesson has the quality of revenge about it rather than compassion.

183

This is a very seductive moment. It is the moment when the sirens call us. If we keep blaming, we will not have to face the loss that we have suffered and mourn it. We will not have to give up hope of a better past.

Forgiving others and ourselves

When we let go of saying things should have been different, we can mourn what happened and move towards forgiveness. We take responsibility and acknowledge that we made the best choice we were able to make and perhaps everyone else did too. That is who we were then. Now that we understand the choices we made, we can do better or different next time. Luckily, we are here to tell the tale. What have we learnt?

It is up to us to learn our own lessons only. Others will learn theirs if and when they are ready.

Before we are able to get to this place of responsibility and forgiveness, we do need to listen to the pain and the rage, to cry and shout and scream if appropriate. That pain and rage are not for nothing. We mustn't deny them again.

A woman I met many years ago gave me this little phrase which I've never forgotten, 'Fuck you – and I put you in God's hands.' She meant: *Yes, I'm angry – but it's not my job to teach you a lesson or make you suffer. Your fate is not in my hands.*

Forgiveness definitely does not mean understanding the other person's point of view so that we don't have a right to ours, nor does it mean condoning the actions of a bully. What it does mean is that we give up on being a victim of what happened. We are choosing to step right up into the twenty-first century and be here. If we have suffered, we don't want to suffer one more minute. We would rather have freedom and love than resentment, self-pity and self-blame. It is the choice to say a Great Yes.

Maya, psychotherapist, one of whose burnout symptoms was a thyroid problem, told me about how her 'No blame' letter to her ex-partner helped in her healing.

I wrote a letter to him and forgave him. I showed it to my friends before I gave it to him to make sure I was taking full responsibility and not blaming. And it's completely released me. I am now ready to move forward. Since then my thyroid problem started to go away. I'd been left choking on something for years, holding on to rage, resentment, blame, tears. I couldn't forgive and couldn't move on. I think I got the thyroid problem when I knew it was time to forgive but didn't want to do it. Finally, I have. But I could only come to the point of no blame when I could.

And while we're at it, why pile up the things to forgive? I am reminded of the time my friend Robin, to my surprise, got angry at me for forgiving him. He told me, 'I don't want you to get angry and blaming, and then forgive me. Why don't you just love me and give me the benefit of the doubt to begin with?'

Why not indeed? We could say to ourselves: *Hey, I probably had a good reason for what I was doing. It just didn't work out. Or anyway it doesn't look like it has worked out. Who knows really? I just don't want to do that again.* We can do the same for others. The more we respect the message of the anger but don't blame, the less resentment, self-pity, self-attack and corrosive criticism we accumulate in our system, the less there is to forgive. It is an easier path.

It is also crucial to healing from burnout that we keep our energy to heal us in the here and now. Every one of those feelings takes more energy than we can afford to give it. If we give up hope of the future and of the past and don't accumulate any more bad feelings for a while, we are doing serious spring-cleaning that creates space and energy for joy and creativity to emerge. Once they do, we won't remember what we couldn't forgive. We wouldn't want things to be any other way.

Forgiving life

The place where our lack of forgiveness is held is not always in our relationship to ourselves or others, but in the feelings we have about life itself. For example, on some hardly conscious level we may have always felt that life never welcomed us, that we are like uninvited guests that have to earn our right to be here. It is like that background feeling of a dream that hangs over us when we wake. We may find that we have the same or a complementary feeling in our relationship to work or intimate partners.

Whatever happened to us while we were burning out will have brought these feelings to the fore. We may be feeling that life has betrayed us or destroyed everything we have worked to build up. We can feel like damaged goods, bereft, angry, hard done by or ashamed. These are probably very familiar feelings that come up for us whenever things go wrong in a particular way.

These feelings often started very early, when our experience of being with mother or father was our whole life. We may now have very different feelings about our parents as people, but the feelings we developed about life itself may still remain. This is why we can transform everything about how we live, yet find that our underlying feelings haven't changed at all, or we can forgive everyone in our life and still feel angry or resentful or self-pitying in some vague, unspecified way. It is these underlying feelings towards life that need healing now.

Conversations about forgiving and being forgiven by life itself can change the underlying tone of day-to-day living and help us to let go of our hopes for a better past in a very profound way. Experiment with the exercise *Forgiving life* under Try This . . . below. You may need to do it again and again as deeper issues emerge.

A conversation with life which really changed things for me comes to mind: I asked life that tormenting question: *Why is it that you always give me everything but the thing I really want?*

Life, like a good Jewish mother, answered a question with a question: *Why is it that whatever I give you, you still complain?*

By the time that conversation was over, I understood just how much I take for granted whatever goes well, and focus on the next problem. I promised to do better. That promise ushered in a beautiful phase of cherishing life with my kids. I recall it with special gratitude because they soon moved out of the house and into their new lives.

During that same rather blessed period, I also went on a long-awaited trip with my friend Naomi in her camper van. Naomi was worried because it was starting to rain. I found myself saying, 'Even a rainy day is a day.'

Nothing is unforgivable

Another benefit of forgiveness is that it reassures us on a deep level that nothing is unforgivable. What drove us forward, against all reason, against all inner whisperings, against reality itself, towards burnout was the fear that if we stopped doing or being or achieving whatever it was, we would be worthless, wicked, selfish, bad. We would not be forgiven.

By forgiving we tell ourselves now and forever: *Nothing you do is unforgivable. There is no need ever to stop listening to yourself or to reality because the truth would be unbearable. Even when you don't listen to the truth, that too is forgivable. It's safe to be honest.*

Keep the faith

We cannot wait and give up hope unless we keep the faith, which means that we trust and we surrender. We are letting go of the structures which have held us safe and which are also the structures that the world around us knows and values. We are losing not only our own personal safety nets, but many of the social ones as well. This can feel very dangerous indeed. Keeping the faith makes the difference between giving up hope and hopelessness.

When burning out, we believed that if we didn't hold it together it would all fall apart – and so would we. We depended on our old ability to control everything, which we sensed was escaping our grasp. Wasn't it all up to us to make it all right? So learning to keep the faith and surrender to it is a hard one for us.

Faith in what?

What is the faith in? This is something I cannot tell you, except to say that probably you would not have got this far in reading this book without there being something that you truly trust in that goes beyond the normal social pictures and plans. It may be God, or your soul, or human love, or persistent hopefulness, or curiosity, or your breath and heartbeat – whatever you feel is constant when all else changes. Why not just trust yourself, the self that has brought you honourably through difficult times to where you are now, maybe feeling awful but still alive and kicking, and that will bring you through again? Whatever you trust, if it depends in any way on your doing or achieving something, it is not going to work. The exercise *If I really trusted you* under Try This . . . below can help you to explore what it is you trust.

Faith or trust is not constant, at least not in our feelings. It requires a decision and a discipline. If you lose the feeling, you can remind yourself of that decision, put your will behind it and show willing.

I surrender

At this moment in our Radical Healing, once we have found even a scent of our own inner trust, it is time to surrender to whatever is greater than our conscious control mind. We surrender to the rhythms of our own body, and also to our heart, nature, love, God, or whatever or whomever we are beginning to trust. As we surrender to our own soul, we have that feeling of coming home.

- Before we burnt out, we gave ourselves away. Now we surrender to something larger than ourselves.
- Before, we tried to hold it all together. Now, we let ourselves be held.
- Before, we ignored our soul's whisperings until it withdrew its support. Now, we have slowed down enough to come home to our soul and to walk in its light.

When we want to surrender but don't know how, it can help simply to bow our heads. When I do that, my mind empties and I feel a sense of awe. It is as if something larger than my normal self is present. If, after bowing my head, I smile, I also become aware of immense gratitude. Here I am, and there is nowhere else I would rather be.

Try This: Forgiving life and/or If I really trusted you.
Forgiving life (and being forgiven too)
- Allow an image to emerge of life and your relationship to it. Imagine life is opposite you, perhaps in an empty chair. How do you feel in its presence?

- Talk to life, saying all the things you feel, including the rage and the fear and the abandonment and whatever else comes up.
- Switch places and become life, and feel what it feels like. Look back at yourself (whom I will call Self). How does Self look to you? Respond to what Self said.
- Go on with this conversation, being brutally honest, until you really acknowledge what each of you needs and are ready to forgive each other. This may take more than one conversation.
- Once you do forgive each other, allow the love to flow between you.

If I really trusted you

- Talk to yourself and say: *Dear (your name), if I really honoured you this is what I would honour you for . . . And if I really trusted you, this is why I would trust you . . .* You could also try, *If I really honoured/trusted life, what would I honour/trust?* Notice the first thought that comes to mind to finish the sentences. If it is something negative or cynical, notice that, let go and continue to surrender.
- Looking back on your life, see and acknowledge what has brought you here, what quality of your being or of life has been trustworthy all these years. Then write down what you have said. Or meditate on 'what I trust', choose colours and draw, letting your fingers tell you where to go. Get some words and/or an image to symbolize this essence of you or of life so that you can call them to mind in times of doubt.
- Now ask yourself: *Am I willing to commit myself to hold to this trust even when I am not feeling it? If so, why?*
- If you make this commitment, and you know why, don't forget when the going gets rough. The exercise *The bubble* under Try This . . . in Chapter 12 can help you to get your will aligned with this commitment.

Finally: All cannot be lost

As you are carried along, you will not know where you are going because you have stopped the control and given up hope. But keep the faith. All cannot be lost. After all, you are still there, breathing.

And each time you start to get a bit of energy back and start making your plans and feeling excited by them, and then getting worried, and then moving into action at great speed because all is not yet lost if you hurry, just remember that little mantra:

Wait. Give up Hope. Keep the Faith.

And take three enjoyable breaths.

Repeat three times for best effect.

12

From Hovel to Palace
Give Your Soul a Good Home

Now that we've learnt to wait, give up hope, keep the faith, and do the listening that is food for our hungry soul, we have a new challenge. We need to give our soul a good home. In Hebrew, the word *hey-chal*[1] means palace or temple. To me this conjures up the perfect home for our soul, and therefore for us.

What if you don't believe we have a soul? You may remember that great advertising slogan, 'You don't need to be Jewish to eat Levi's bread'. You don't need to believe in a soul to have a sense of interior majesty. What we call the human spirit, which is a way of talking about our aspirations, our courage, our ability to survive and contribute, is just as deserving of reverence. If we can feel awe at the wondrous quality of an oak tree or a nightingale or the Grand Canyon, we don't need to be spiritual to feel awe about our human beingness.

In this chapter we will be seeking to answer the question: How do we create the best inner environment in which to heal and to find a new way forward?

- Before, we filled our world with beautiful contributions; now, we empty the space so that we have room to breathe and to laugh.
- Before, we used our creativity to achieve; now, we discipline ourselves to work without looking for results.
- Before, we were trying to create a better world out there; now, we begin by offering a better home for our own soul.

Creating a good home for our soul doesn't mean that we have given up on contributing, being creative, working towards a better world. But instead of driving ourselves to fulfil a purpose, we are creating a space in which our authentic purpose, energy and joy feel safe enough to show themselves and guide us to our next step.

Palaces and hovels

When I think of that Hebrew word *hey-chal*, palace and temple in one, I think of a vast resounding space, with beautiful marble floors and temple bells sounding. Along with its grandeur, there is a warmth about it, and the feeling that people laugh, dance and sing here. It makes me want to throw myself down, breathe gratitude and surrender. This is my image of the inner space of our lives at its best.

There is an old saying that 'Philosophers build beautiful palaces and live in the hovel next door.' We actually live in the palace or temple but turn it into a hovel within moments. We act like insensitive tourists, marching around, knocking things down as we go, taking photos of the best views, preparing what we will tell our friends. We are disappointed that it is not as grand as we think it should be and consider how we can spruce it up so it is in fashion. We are certain that other people have greater and better palaces than ours, and shrink in shame that ours isn't good enough.

We look around, and all of a sudden, the palace looks small and dingy. It has become a hovel, just as we always thought it was. This is what we deserve.

Bargaining

If we are burnt out, our palace or temple is by now pretty neglected and hovel-like. So what do we need to do to create and maintain a beautiful temple or palace? In one of my meditations, this single principle came to me as the one I needed to follow if I wanted my life to be a *hey-chal*:

You need to decide that there is nothing that will make you happy that you don't already have.

I bargained immediately: *But first I need a good relationship. But first I need a publisher for my book.* No exclusion clauses were allowed.

I thought long and hard about whether I could honour this commitment. As I did so, I realized how much I have unconsciously assumed that my real life is somewhere else, and that when I find it, I will be okay.

When my kids were being born I swore that if they were born healthy I would be happy and never worry again. They were, thank God, and I didn't keep the promise.

So, I knew I had to agree to this principle. The practice was not always so easy. One thing after another surreptitiously slipped into centre stage as the thing I needed in order to be happy. The minute there was a drive towards *having* to have something in order to be okay, my *hey-chal* became a train station, my joy disappeared, and the train to burnout signalled *All aboard*.

But each time I remembered that principle, I would smile. Caught out again. Time to recommit to my *hey-chal*. As I did, my joy streamed back as if by magic.

I would love myself unconditionally if only I were different
Margaret, teacher, wrote me about how she used to see herself:

> *My image of myself was that I had to be completely responsible for and to everyone to whom I committed myself. I had to work hard, be competitive, more than who I was, because otherwise I would not be good enough. I depended on others for positive feedback, and feared criticism. I feared I would not be loved.*

These sentiments are echoed, in one form or another, by most of the burnout people I have known. We knew that these attitudes weren't really good for us but we had them anyway. We worried, criticized ourselves, told ourselves how we 'should be', tried to please people and be over-responsible for them, and generally drove ourselves crazy.

All these attitudes are related to thinking that something could make us happy that we don't already have. As long as we are trying to get to our happiness somewhere else, we are subject to self-attack for not being there and worry about whether we will get there at all. We will feel that things should be different and escape into fantasy rather than living in reality. We will ignore our physical signals, become resentful and angry and depressed about what we are missing, try to fix everyone and everything up and fear that if we don't they will fall apart. And we will wish we were anywhere else but here.

In other words, we will do all the things we know we have to stay away from, like an addict from a fix. And we will be unable to surrender to the present moment, because it is imperfect. I once wrote an article entitled *I would love myself unconditionally if only I were different*. It's a bit like that.

Discipline

Here another word comes in that I feel is crucial: *Discipline*. With all this letting go and letting be, this may be surprising. Discipline means that besides all the inner listening and emotional work, there is also a decision just to do what's good for us. When I asked Doris, accountant, the main principle of how she got well from burnout, she said, '*I decided to.*'

Just as before we engaged our will wholeheartedly behind what we loved or found meaningful or necessary, now we need to engage that will equally wholeheartedly to construct our inner home. We won't always feel like it or see the sense of it any more than we always felt like going to work or taking care of the kids. But we still have to do it.

Phil, insurance broker, spoke of how much he needed his discipline:

> If I take away the discipline, I don't pay attention and I don't do T'ai Chi or meditation, and I stop sticking to my diet and checking in with myself and working openheartedly. I soon get miserable and depressed. As long as I'm constant I feel a sense of realness, a wholesomeness. I eat something and I feel good, and I can enjoy something and let it go and look forward to the next thing, I don't need to have the big alcohol hits. I actually enjoy doing what is also healthy for me.

Think of this as a new form of achievement you can get your teeth into. But, and this is a very big but, this discipline is not a forcing of ourselves into a mould. It is not our control mind ordering us to get ourselves sorted and perfect. The old driven way will drive us right back to bed, lying prone and unable to do anything.

It is more like a deep decision to ask our will to align itself behind our intention, and then stepping back while it does. 'Okay,' we say, 'I am reporting for duty.' *The bubble* exercise from Try This . . . below is great for making things happen in this new way.

As with any form of disciplined exercise, we cannot expect miracles the minute we start our programme. We will not have big muscles after a day at the gym, or a quiet mind after one meditation session. But we *will* have a bit more trust in our own ability to do what is good for us.

We have to work without looking for results.

And we must remember to honour ourselves each time we keep to our commitment. The results come as and when they will. Only the discipline is up to us.

Bodies

We cannot create an inner space and ignore the outer expression of it – our bodies. Whether or not we had any interest in caring for our bodies before we burnt out, I and all the burnout people I have known developed some kind of body–mind discipline. It might be a form of diet or T'ai Chi or yoga or working out or breathwork or walking, or whatever is our thing.

Many of us started having regular consultations with a variety of health practitioners, Chinese herbalists or body–mind workers. Most of us felt that working with our body by ourselves or with professionals was crucial to recovering from burnout. For some of us, it meant changing our old identity as people who had our mind on the 'higher' things and thought our bodies would take care of themselves if we just fed them and clothed them and took them out for a walk every now and then.

Some of us needed to spend a period in a beautiful place where it was possible to walk, swim, indulge the senses or be part of nature. Others actually moved somewhere where nature was more accessible and having a physical life didn't require driving to a gym. We needed to reconnect not only to an inner sense of our body but to the feeling that our body was part of the natural world.

Friendly reminders

Often, if the burnout has left physical after-effects, our bodies will be sending us messages every time we go in the wrong direction. When our energy is very low, we can literally feel it every time we even have a thought that is not about being here right now. Leila, retreat director, echoed this:

> When I was at my most delicate I had that sense that one negative thought would hurt my body. It was like seeing this map of how the emotions and thoughts affect the body.

Carl, the manager whose story was told in Chapter 1, said:

> I'm very well and I still have limitations in my body – the symptoms of chronic fatigue are still present when I overdo things – a kind of friendly reminder. I am healed in my heart but the truth is I have to be very careful about my activity level and careful about balance in my life. It is an ongoing challenge. But it is a kind of friendly challenge. I don't see it as limiting. I see it as a friend who is helping me to look after myself. That is not to say that I don't feel cheesed off when I get symptoms.

The secret with all these physical symptoms is to be aware of their message but not to worry about them or think we'll never get better. Worry and fear always make symptoms worse. Take care, but don't worry. The more stillness there is in our attitude, the quicker we can heal.

At a time when I was quite ill with the effects of my burnout, I was taking a trip from London to California and was seriously worried about whether I would manage the stress of that trip. I suddenly understood: *I need to be completely still on the plane. I'm not going anywhere. California will come to me.* And of course it did.

Loving our body from the inside

There are plenty of recipes for how to take care of and be with our body. The inner attention and love we give to our bodies will lead us to the best approach for us. It is not the perfect body we seek, but the love for the wonders of being a body.

In the past, what we did to support our body was often in the service of where we were going and what we were achieving. Even our ways of exercising our body could be harsh and goal-oriented. Then in driving ourselves to burn out, we overrode our natural balance, damaged our energy system, and in many cases became ill. Now our body has said, *Stop, take care of me, but in service of me.*

I remember a moment when I was suffering what felt like a dark night of the soul. I had let go of so much of my life and work that I knew that the world could manage without me and now I couldn't remember the point of just living. I lay in bed, feeling really dead, as if the spirit had left my body.

Then it was as if I heard a whisper inside saying, *You must go back.* I asked *Why?* The answer came, *You have work to do.* My response was, *No, I'm not going back for that.* Then I heard, *So you can love your body from the inside.* My spirit just popped back into my body.

Yes, no, please, thank you

When we are recovering from burnout, we tend to have a fear that we will lose all the old standards from that social world we were once successful in, perhaps become unrecognizable, unacceptable and morally lax. Our clothes and our pastimes will be a sure sign that we have fallen between the cracks. And we may indeed face such criticism from people around us.

It may feel rather like 'going native', that tendency which representatives of the former British Empire sometimes had of beginning to dress and live like the people in the country they were supposed to be 'ruling'. It was associated with losing all 'standards', and being unacceptable to the society they used to inhabit. The idea that the people native to the country had a culture worth respecting would have been impossibly threatening to those looking on and judging.

Creating a good home for our soul includes creating a space around us that doesn't allow those criticisms, views and demands to enter in. It is as if when we enter into our palace and shut the door, no one is allowed in, especially not the critical voices we carry around in our heads.

The challenge of doing this is huge. We are living in a world that can feel very stressed, threatening and dangerous, and it is easy to mirror this in our inner world. And yet just as a parent can seek to create as good a home as they can for their precious children despite war and devastation, so we can do our best to create a protected inner home whatever else is going on out there or in our control minds.

No, no, no

Perhaps you could imagine in your mind a kind of chalk circle in which you walk around just saying NO NO NO NO NO NO NO and pushing out with your hands and arms so that you have a big space around you. This is no to criticism, to demands, to shoulds and should nots, to feelings of failure and not being good enough, to old rules, to old fears, to anything and anyone that don't make you and your soul expand in delight. Love and warmth go in and out without obstruction. But any expectations or demands, whether they come from you or from others, are immediately halted.

No is of course the great boundary setter, and the hardest for us burnout people to say. No says that whatever it is the world wants or seems to need is not right for me to offer right now. No also says that it is not my job to rescue you. It may help to remind ourselves or someone else: *This is a refusal, not a rejection.*

If your sense of someone else or their expectations of you feels particularly intrusive, so that you cannot keep their face or presence out even in your imagination, and the nos don't seem to work, try the exercise *Taking back my energy* from Try This . . . in Chapter 6. Pull back all the energy you have invested. It is *your* energy and you need every last bit of it to re-establish that energy flow that has got so out of balance.

Yes, yes, yes

There is another way to create that space around us, and that is with a YES. If we come back to our true self and our true radiance, we are always centred and safe. With all that positive energy radiating, it is difficult for anything harmful to us to penetrate our energy field. This is what healers do so as not to take in the problems of those they are healing. If we send out a powerful love force from our being, the outside world cannot just collapse into us.

When we are burnt out we tend to be so depleted that it is difficult to remember our natural radiance. We easily feel invaded by other people's thoughts and feelings and our own old critical voices. Try the exercise *Breathing and expanding* under Try This . . . in Chapter 10 again, to imagine your radiance expanding.

It is always a good basic principle to expand whenever there is a problem. What happens when we get stressed rather than stretched by a situation is that we contract. If we keep in mind that each time we face what seems impossible we need to expand rather than contract, we will find a lot more resources available to us. How would I experience this if I expanded? If I stepped into a bigger picture, what would it be? What if my radiance filled the world, how would it be? Remember:

Expand don't contract

More generally, YES, said as a Great Yes, is an affirmation that this is something I truly want or want to do and I will put my will behind it. I say Yes to my own health and happiness and wholeheartedness in doing it. It is sometimes a Yes to a new way of being me that I've said No to in the past. Judith, management consultant, talked about this:

> *I can't remember all the times something was presented to me and I'd say no because of my old way of looking at the world, and then it came back again and I knew it was what I needed to do. 'Oh, this is the same thing. I'd better say yes.'*

YES and NO depend on each other. If we can't say the one wholeheartedly, we can't say the other wholeheartedly.

Thank you, sorry

While we're on the small words, there are two more good ones. THANK YOU says that we don't take what we receive for granted, but that if we do receive something we don't have to deserve it or pay it back. *Whether or not I deserve this, thank you.* SORRY says that we don't have to get it right or else feel humiliated, avoid or lie. We can acknowledge the truth and ask forgiveness.

Space to breathe

All these small words say to your work, your partner, your friend, your family or life or God: *You and I are separate from each other, even though on another level we may all be one. What I give, I give freely. What I receive, I receive gratefully. I already have and am enough. When I am needlessly hurtful, I apologize. But I don't apologize for being my true self or for taking care of myself.*

This counteracts old principles which may have been: *I am part of you and I give everything to you, and in exchange you should give me everything I want. I need a lot because I am so neglected – by myself. And I mustn't get it wrong, or fail to be perfect, or I will be so very ashamed. I should, you should, we all should, and then it will all be okay.*

Each time we set better boundaries around ourselves, we decrease our need to manipulate other people. They don't have to be how we want them to be, or feel towards us as we'd like them to. It is enough that we have our own space to appreciate being ourselves in.

We do what we want to do

In this inner world, we follow this simple principle that is a crucial one for us burnout people:

I do what I want to do and not what I don't want to do.

Once, this would have seemed the height of selfishness or laziness. Now, we understand it is a way of honouring our true self. It doesn't work when we are addicted to something, but it does when we are in our clear free space. What we want to do is what we want to do. Why ever not?

I remember when I saw for the first time that I was like someone beating a donkey and saying, 'Work, damn you, work.' My main assumption was that the donkey was lazy and inadequate, and unless it was beaten it wouldn't do what it was supposed to do. At that moment it occurred to me that maybe I could assume the donkey was all right as it was, and find out about how it was for the donkey. What did this donkey want to do?

The thought was revolutionary. If I was tired, I didn't need to figure out why I was so tired and attack myself for it. I just had to rest. If I had a phone call to make but I felt I couldn't do another thing, I could stop. As my energy flowed back, I would find myself walking over to the phone. After all, I *wanted* to do it. Otherwise, why do it?

Doing what delights us is what will light our fires and nourish the part of us that is languishing right now. If we don't know how, we need to take time to experiment. Do also try the exercise *It's the end of the day* under Try This . . . below to help clarify what you really want.

Anything that brings us energy and recharges us is now a must, not an extra when the work is done. This *is* our work, in the sense that we take our play as seriously and wholeheartedly as children do.

This is an especially wonderful time for increasing intimacy, with friends, with family, with lovers. Now we have time or have made time to play, we can open up on a deeper and more real level. Anne, university lecturer, told me:

> One good thing about burning out was that it led to more orgasms! When I was running around, trying to do well at work, going to the gym, worrying whether my partner was okay, trying to be the perfect sexual partner, I never had the energy, the time or even the interest to find out what sex was about for me. Now I do, and it's great.

What depends on me?

As we discipline ourselves to do what is good for us and avoid what is not good for us, we cannot help but begin to feel differently about ourselves and about life. There is a shift in how we choose to spend our time, with the emphasis on the word 'choose', since in the pre-burnout period most of our choices were really prioritizing which obligation to meet first. Janey, health consultant and editor, said:

Every minute of the day was crammed with things and that included my personal life as well. Now it is much more open. Even though I have more time now, paradoxically I'm beginning to think much more about conscious choices of who I spend my time with – who do I really feel like seeing.

Time feels more elastic. It's possible to have different rhythms within a day or even over a longer time. I have the freedom to ask myself what I'd like to do, which includes doing nothing. Before, this was not a question you could afford to ask yourself. The job and other people's demands always came first.

We begin to be unwilling simply to go on doing what is best for others and not including ourselves in the picture. And when we find we are losing our way, we notice, and do something about it. Julie, arts organization director, told me:

Now I am much more content. I have things I want to do with my life, so I don't have time to rescue everyone else – they can rescue themselves.

Last year, when I lost my ability to sleep and my symptoms started coming back, I immediately stopped everything and went into hospital. This time I was able to stop the roundabout and step off. And I quite enjoyed myself – no mobile phone, crisp white sheets, people bringing food. Knowing your own stress triggers and dealing with your own distress is crucial. And the world didn't collapse. We missed out on one major project, but so what? We'll do it again next year.

There is a gradual shift in responsibility – from feeling the world depends on us to feeling that how we live depends on us. Margaret, teacher, said:

I learnt I could not drive myself that hard or I would not be able to live my life. I learnt it was most important that I be responsible for myself, be more receptive, more easy with myself, allow myself to BE, not DO all the time. These lessons continue with my work with

*breath, which moves me. I wanted to be a dancer all my life and
now my breath dances me.*

By following her breath, Margaret also found her vocation in the
field of breathwork. She is now doing what she loves.

Try This: The end of the day and/or The bubble

The end of the day:

We don't always know what we really want to do. One way to
find out is to put ourselves at the end of the day, the hour, the
party, the meeting or whatever and look back:

- Say to yourself: *It's the end of the day/hour/event and I
  feel good. What's the good feeling?* As you say this, let
  yourself actually be in the future and feel that feeling.
  Don't let your control mind have a say. Don't even figure
  out why you are feeling that way. First find the feeling.
- Now, ask yourself: *What is the main thing I feel good
  about?*
- Now, look back as if you are remembering that day, hour
  or event. What did I do that got me here?
- To get this even clearer, you can add: It's the end of the
  day/hour/event and I feel bad. Follow the same principles.
  Then notice what is the essential difference.
- *The bubble* exercise below can help you make the future
  you want happen with minimum effort.

The bubble:

Thinking constantly about what we should be doing or feeling
is an energy killer. This little exercise helps whenever there is
something we want to feel or do. It gets the intention or plan
off that race track running around our minds and into the
realm of potential waiting to actualize itself. I would give this
exercise top rating as a burnout person's new way to get
things done. And it doesn't take more than a minute or two.

- Picture yourself having the feeling you want or doing

---

whatever it is that needs doing, or better still, having done it already, see/feel what that is like. Breathe into that sense of being there.

- Then put that picture in a bubble, and say to yourself: *I ask and intend for this to be.* As you say so feel that real willingness you have to open yourself up to this, a true wholeheartedness.
- Then, let the bubble waft off and you might add, *And I release it.* That means that we can't make it happen nor does it have to happen. We can only ask that this be and then let it go.
- Then take that feeling you put in the bubble, breathe it inside you and feel it for a moment. As you feel it, it is good to add: *Thank you. It is already so.*
- Now wait for what unfolds. Watch and see whether, when your energy flows back or when the time is right, you find yourself doing or feeling what you pictured.

Finally: When the joy begins to flow in

If we create a beautiful home for the soul, the soul will naturally create a beautiful life for us and for others. And we don't have to deserve it. **Joy is the free gift of the soul. It is literally the love of our life.** Carol, health consultant, told me:

When I eliminated my life for the life of the work I found that the joy began to leave the work. It was no longer a pleasure. When I gave the joy back to my life it came back to the work. So one feeds the other.

I've now given myself permission to do the things I love and I realize that they are as important as anything I do in the world. Before, I felt I had something to prove. I had to earn my right to be here. Now, I know it's my right just to be here. I don't have to earn it at all.

13

The Truth Hurts but It Doesn't Harm
Build Up Your 'Living Truthfully Muscle'

I've often thought of life as being a bit like a double-exposure photo –
two pictures next to each other, one of how I am now, and one of how
I should be, vying for the focus. Living truthfully is about letting those
two pictures dissolve into one focus. *This is me. This is now.*

When we were burning out, one of the things we did was ignore the
messages from our bodies, the discomfort in our emotions, the
whispering of our soul in favour of our picture of how we should
be and how things should be. Now we're on the path of Radical
Healing, we've started to reconnect to what is real and true. This
chapter addresses the question of what it means to live truthfully,
what it doesn't mean, and why we should bother to do this most
difficult thing.

The first step in living truthfully is to decide once and for all to
commit ourselves to putting truth first. But then, hour by hour and
day by day, in the supermarket or in the bedroom or in the board-
room, we have to take our heart in our hands and reaffirm that truth
continues to be our first choice. This is how we build up our flabby
'living truthfully muscle'.

Living truthfully doesn't mean never telling a lie

When I talk to people about living truthfully, it raises all kinds of fears
about what it might mean. So let me start with what living truthfully
isn't:

- Living truthfully doesn't mean never telling a lie. That said, as we continue to live truthfully, we have less interest in telling lies. Nothing seems so important that we want to perjure ourselves for it.
- Living truthfully doesn't mean going around and telling everyone we meet everything we think and feel. Discretion can be more honest than confession.
- It is not about giving up playing any roles. When I am teaching, I have a different purpose and different parts of me emerge than when I am having a coffee with a friend. We can still be authentically ourselves whatever role we are playing.
- Nor is it about giving up our social responsibility and just letting it all hang out and following our whims. Loving and being responsible is an aspect of being true to ourselves.
- Nor does living truthfully mean the Absolute Objective Truth. It is about the absolute best we can do at a given moment if we free ourselves from whatever gets in the way.
- Living truthfully is not about what our control minds tell us to do or believe. It is about the a messages from our bodies and from our whole being.

What is living truthfully?

Living truthfully is based on this commitment:
   I **put my true self first and everything else second**.

Being honest with ourselves
It starts with the intention to be honest with ourselves about our own experience. When a deep fault-line opens up in our life, as it did at the moment we started to go on that burnout trail, we will not tell ourselves our spectacles are cracked. We will stop and listen to what we know but haven't told ourselves. We will trust that whatever it is can be honoured and allowed to unfold.

Phil, insurance broker, told me how he knew what is true:

It's quite easy. It's like hitting a ball in the middle of a racket. I know the truth because it feels like a melting. It feels warm. That sweet sensation of truth. And it's coupled with love, unconditional love. I find if I am dealing with myself in that way, I am dealing with other people in that way.

Our old dishonesty with ourselves reached into every corner of our lives. For burnout people, everyday dealings with time are a particularly good breeding ground for dishonesty. Each time we say, 'I'll be there/do that/see you in five minutes' because we are afraid to tell the truth that it is more likely to be ten or fifteen, we are choosing to please someone or our own critical voices rather than to live truthfully. Each time we spend two hours with someone because we didn't dare say we wanted to go after one hour, we are being economical with the truth. Even wishing for more than twenty-four hours in a day because *then* we could get it all done is a kind of dishonesty. It implies that we could or should be doing more than our best.

Ellen, management consultant, talked of her work contracts:

We took on work that paid too little and was based on our estimating too few hours of work. Then we'd honour our commitment to high standards by working way overtime. Now I'd start with myself and ask whether the work was right for me at this point in time. And then I'd be clearer about the contract and how to make it work for the best but within the reality of the circumstances. And I'd have more courage to speak my truth faster when discrepancies arise.

Knowing and being our true self with others

Living truthfully continues as the willingness to know and be our true selves wherever we go and whatever we do. It is about a profound intimacy, the feeling that I have nothing to hide, so that I can really be me with you, and you can be you with me. And, for that matter, I can be me with me. This is one of the great joys of living truthfully.

Mary, airline planner, spoke about how her new life and new

relationships were about honesty with herself and with her new lover.

> *In my new relationship I just won't allow myself to think what's not true. I'm not in control of the relationship – it will unfold as it unfolds and I'm quite content with that. The most important thing is that I'm being honest with myself.*

Taking responsibility for what is ours and not for what isn't is part of being ourselves. When we don't, we create a mess around us that confuses and hurts everyone. So when things go wrong, we need to be honest about our part in it, and clear about how we saw the role of the other. For those of us who are inveterate rescuers, this is about letting others feel their feelings and not fixing them. For those of us who are inveterate blamers, it is about knowing that throwing around blame just creates more defensiveness and conflict, and is usually less than half the truth.

It helps a lot if we surround ourselves intimately with people who want us to know our truth, who care enough to hear it, and are willing to confront their own truths. We can recognize people who are not so inclined by the way we feel out of touch and in some kind of role when we are with them. When we are with someone who lives a false self, or are in an environment with a false facade, it is almost impossible to stay true ourselves. We get sucked into the vortex of illusion.

Being there

Living truthfully is above all about being there, our ability to stay present to ourselves and to other people. Most of the time, our sense of self gets knocked out as we rush around worrying, pleasing, striving, doing, getting high and getting low, criticizing ourselves and others, and generally trying to be there for the world but not for ourselves. Woody Allen once said, 'I don't mind dying as long as I don't have to be there.' When we were on that burnout trail, we had a similar attitude about living: *It's a great life; I just wish I didn't have to be there making it happen.*

Maxine, former head-hunter who is now a management coach, told me:

When I see other people who are on the edge of burnout or trapped in jobs they hate, they are only half there when you talk to them. They are not present. When we're distracted and cluttered inside, there just isn't room for other people.

When we do learn to hang on in there, knowing that our full presence is more important than anything we are worried about, we begin to re-own the lives that we've been alienated from. Thich Nhat Hanh, or Thay, tells a story about being introduced to a man who had only a few weeks to live. Thay just said, 'A few weeks? So many minutes? Good. Let's have a cup of tea.' As they had a cup of tea together, fully present, the man had a kind of enlightenment experience. And he is still alive.

Knowing and doing

Putting truth first has two aspects: knowing the truth, and then doing something about it. It probably sounds as if these just follow as the day does the night – if you know what's true, you have to do something about it.

It is actually better to keep these aspects separate in our minds. Dare to know the truth, and then wait and see what you do. Many burnout people feared to listen to their own truth and save themselves because they thought that if they stopped and listened they would have to do something about it which they didn't want to do.

This little saying I learnt as a child sums it up for me: *I hate spinach and I'm glad I hate spinach because if I liked it I would eat it and I hate spinach.*

Building up our flabby 'living truthfully muscle'

Our ability to live truthfully is like a muscle that is flabby unless we exercise it. Those of us who burn out must by definition have living truthfully muscles that were too weak for our purposes. When we came to the crunch, and when our soul was whispering to us that the old ways were not working, we were unable to stop and listen, and we were unable to follow. Our living truthfully muscle wasn't strong enough to make a different decision.

When our living truthfully muscle is weak, other muscles take over. They tell us *Not yet, Just this one last time, I can't possibly* or *Please don't make me change.* Each time we refuse to follow these voices and consciously honour our truth, we strengthen our living truthfully muscle.

As we do so, we take back more of our sense of self. The next time we face a choice, we have more self to make that choice with. We have a better idea of who and what we are, and greater trust in our ability to be honest with ourselves, and to do what nourishes us. This bigger sense of self is what so many of us burnout people are probably most grateful for having gained.

The truth may hurt

At the heart of why we maintain so many illusions about ourselves or about life is the belief that we could avoid pain by being, doing, believing, having whatever it is. It is hard to accept this simple truth:

It hurts to be human and it is human to hurt. We cannot avoid pain, but the pain of not being ourselves is, in the end, far greater.

Often, at least in our minds, the hurt we fear is someone else's. Countless times over my years of people-work, clients or students have come up against a truth and their first fear was about who might be hurt by it – a parent, a partner, a boss or a child. Someone else had to be protected. And each time I have had to say:

The truth may hurt but it doesn't harm. It is illusions that can kill.

The pain of truth is always healing. Like painfully cleaning out a wound, we are starting a process towards joy. The pain of illusion just goes on and on because it is keeping us stuck in destructive patterns.

Our omnipotent illusions about ourselves nearly finished us off. There are people whose illusions make them willing to finish off someone else. Protecting other people's illusions have put us at risk. Mass illusions are endangering the earth. Illusions are not a safe playing field. The road to burnout is paved with our and other people's illusions.

Whatever it is we tell others, at least we need to be honest with ourselves. Mary, airline planner, told me about the truths she had to face:

I had to admit everything I'd been avoiding. Surrendering to the fact that I didn't like my job, that it hadn't been good for me for quite some time. I had to let the hurt and fears about all the relationships come through. It was hurt I'd never allowed myself to feel because I thought I had to hold myself together and carry on. No, I don't want it. It is crap. None of it was good for me.

When we confront an illusion we hold dear, we feel pain and loss. But we will have the chance to find more of our selves, be more present, be more real. We will not be harmed. And nor, in my view, will others. In the long run, no one benefits by living with unreality and it is not up to us to decide that someone else cannot stand the truth. What they do with it is up to them.

For Jack, banking lawyer, the turning-point in moving from burnout to healing was when his wife told him a painful truth about his relationship with his six-year-old daughter:

One night Maria said, 'You know, Janet doesn't want to be with you. She's frightened of you.' I was so horrified that it was like an electric shock.

He immediately decided on a few changes. These seemingly small steps were revolutionary for him.

On a practical level, I decided that on Friday evenings I would walk out of the office at six, that I would work less at home so I had more time with the family, and that I would just be more relaxed.

I am not saying it is our job to tell people the truth 'for their own good'. The urge to do so is rife with mixed motives, including needs for control and even revenge, along with a true desire to be of service. We tell the truth if we decide that we need to do so for our own good, for our own ability to live in alignment with our true selves. If we are telling it to someone else for their own good, it almost certainly isn't.

The truth may be joyful

Living truthfully is not all super-serious. It's not just about confronting your pain, saying a difficult no, leaving a relationship or a job in which you are not being treated with respect, or deciding that you may have to do without that future you desperately wanted.

It can be about joyfully coming out with being who you are, and inviting others to join in. It can mean daring to leave behind the old professional straitjackets and overnice ways and going out to play. When I asked Maxine whether she was living more truthfully now, she said an enthusiastic yes. Her first example was this great party.

> Salsa is one of my latest passions. I wanted to share that love with my friends. So I invited all sorts of people who didn't know each other, including my parents. And the men had fake moustaches and the women had little miniature roses that they could put in their hair or their dresses and the food was wonderful Spanish cuisine. A friend offered to do the food – normally when I have parties I do it all and this time it was effortless. And I invited my salsa teacher and I asked her to teach the group for an hour. So she got everyone paired up and got people to move around so by the end of the evening everyone had danced with everyone and different conversations were struck. When I watched people's faces, it was sensational.
>
> Now one couple are going out who weren't going out before, and some people took up salsa, and a singing group is being planned, and my mother asked my friend who did the catering to cater for her eightieth birthday party. Since I feel that cooking is my friend's true calling – it makes her heart sing like coaching makes mine sing – I am hoping that maybe that will draw her to do more of it. I felt I was giving everyone so much pleasure and it was just so satisfying to do it by concentrating on my social life rather than on my work.

Letting go, letting in

What do we need to let go of in order to live truthfully? Every one of our investments is based on the illusion that without this we or our world will not survive intact. It therefore feels more important than the truth. Every addiction is a way we compromise with living out of alignment with ourselves by giving ourselves a treat – and something extra to lie about. Each of these investments and addictions has to go, one by one, if we want to live truthfully.

We do not have to lose everything to prove the point, like Job. But, on some level, we need to be willing to do so if this is what our truth shows us to be the way forward. We need to be free of anything that we need more than the truth – anything that would prevent us from saying a Great Yes or a Great No.

It's a question of building up that living truthfully muscle. How do we do it?

- We recognize an investment that is keeping us from facing the truth.
- We penetrate below the surface of our defences and face all the feelings and pictures that keep our investments in place.
- We care for ourselves really well while we do it.
- When we are able to, we let go of our old pictures, open to a bigger perspective, locate our truth and go with it.
- Then we resist all the messages that tell us that we used to be nicer or better coming from people who have a vested interest in us being as we used to be.

Whenever we give up an investment or an addiction, it feels like a sacrifice. But there is an old spiritual law that once we have gone through the experience of sacrifice, if we are willing to stand empty, we will get back so much more than we could ever have imagined.

We need to face the withdrawal symptoms before we can begin to find out that life tastes a lot better without our fantasies. We need to let go of our specialness to find out the wonders of being 'ordinary'.

Phil hated letting go of the Phil he was before he got ill, and talked about the effect of his refusal to face this truth.

I was seen as this Phil who could do whatever he set out to do, and I liked that. I had about a year of trying to come back to the person I was, and the hardest thing was letting go of that identity. Part of the problem is that there is a depression that comes with it. And on top of the depression you start denying, you feel angry, you feel you deserve some comfort and then you do things that are harmful for you.

But letting go of his old picture gave him a bigger one.

Now, I'm Phil in a more wholesome sense. I have more inner strength than I had because I've noticed my insides more. I've been with myself in a gentler way, equally strong, but in a different way. I'm more balanced. I'm more aware of the part of me that I didn't have a relationship with, the quieter, gentler, more compassionate side.

When I asked Jack, to go back and experience from the inside how it was to be the driven person he used to be, he saw the effect of all his perfectionist ideas about how he should be.

I'm feeling amazed that I could have had those perfectionist views. I'm noticing my abnormal behaviour, the addiction, and how out of touch I was with my core values. The fear of not being in control made me insecure and I went to my limits to feel safe. I'm seeing the deep unhappiness that I wasn't aware of then and I'm feeling horror at the total loss of reality.

As a result of his burnout, Jack went through a painful process of letting go of his need for control and perfection. Having done so, he became able to accept himself as he actually was and begin to enjoy life.

I've realized that by putting all this pressure on myself I was creating the most tremendous amount of unhappiness within myself and in people around me. Rather than work being enjoyable, and running being enjoyable, and being with the family enjoyable, I was so committed to the road to perfection that nothing was enjoyable.

Every burnout person I have known has found this ancient law of sacrifice working in their lives: if they fully let go of whatever was keeping them on that burnout trail and opened up to what was real and true, something bigger and more nourishing flowed into their lives. It was not really a sacrifice, though it looked like it at the time. People who still kept a secret from themselves about how important an investment was, perhaps colluding with an abusive relationship or not daring to face someone's disapproval, did not became fully free.

Living perfectly truthfully is already an illusion

We burnout types tend to think that the achievement, the golden eggs, the perfection of the product are proof that we have got it right. But if we think of living truthfully as something we can achieve once and for all and do perfectly, we have just added a new 'should' to the pile of 'shoulds' that are burning us out already. None of us can live truthfully all the time.

Hour by hour and day by day we have to test the cold light of reality against the warm temperature of our being and find out where we stand. Any reappearing symptoms can be a clue. Elaine, a psychotherapist in private practice, talked of how feeling depleted is her sign that she has stopped being honest.

I have frequently experienced my old feelings of being drained and tired while working with clients and what I have discovered is that it is like an obstruction of energy . . . a 'stuck' feeling. Often, I realize I am sitting on my feelings or not sharing my truth about what I experience going on.

The notion that we can do it perfectly is an illusion and a false pride. We will undoubtedly fail again and again and know it when we bump up against a wall we told ourselves was no longer there. This is hard for us perfectionists. Yet this failure is necessary because we need to keep doing what is slightly outside our limits. This is how we exercise our living truthfully muscle. If we keep going, we are guaranteed success, in the sense that in the long run we get stronger and stronger.

It is only a matter of time. And time doesn't matter.

And this is crucial: no blame. We are not expected to be better than we are. We don't have to be body-builders with the perfectly toned living truthfully muscle; we can just be ordinary guys exercising a little each day. As with any muscle, one over-vigorous workout can set us back for ages.

One truth a day keeps the doctor away. Too many truths could land us in the Emergency Ward. That's not necessarily a bad thing, but perhaps a little drastic?

Try This: Am I willing?

But how do we start living truthfully? We begin by deciding if we are willing. Try this exercise:

- Imagine that you are walking up a hill, and then down the hill and into a valley, and then through a wood and up to a lake. Take your time imagining the feeling, sights and colours of each of these environments, until you feel completely steeped in that world rather than in this everyday world.

- Now imagine that right there in front of you is your House of Truth. Let it arise and emerge before you. What does it look like? As you stand on the doorstep, tell the House of Truth why you are here, and reveal anything that frightens you.

- Imagine becoming the House of Truth, and actually step physically into that place where that House is. How does it feel to be the House of Truth? What is your essential quality? Look back at yourself, whom I will call Self. How does Self look to you?

- Go back to being yourself and enter the House. How do you feel inside? What can you see?

- Now notice in the corner, emerging out of shadows you hadn't noticed, a well with a cover on it. This is the Well of Illusion. Take the cover off and sink the bucket down into the Well and bring up something that represents your

---

main illusion at this moment in your life. What is it? If you bring up an object and don't understand what it means, you can become the object and speak to Self about what your essence is. You might also try putting it up to the light and see what happens when the light shines through it.

- Notice in another part of the room, also in the shadows but coming into view, a throne. This is the Throne of Truth. Sit on this throne, and as if from the seat, allow the main truth that you need to know right now to emerge. What is It?

- The truth and illusion you have been shown are an example of a choice you have to make if you are to live truthfully. What is the choice? Are you willing to make that choice now?

- Kneel and surrender. Consider whether you are willing in your life to commit yourself to know the truth to the best of your ability, and to live by it, whatever the price. Before you agree, consider what it may mean, and what the most difficult thing for you to do will be. Now choose.

- Whichever choice you made, rise now. The House may give you a gift as you go. What is it?

- As you stand outside on the doorstep, look back and find out what the House is saying to you. Say what you want to say to the House and then thank it. Know you can go back any time. There is also a consultant there and a healer whom you haven't yet met. If you want to, you can meet them next time.

- Reflect on what has happened.

Each time, you visit your House of Truth, you will find different illusions and different truths. Our ingenuity for deceiving ourself is, after all, one of the most truly unlimited things about us.

Finally: Socrates and the pig

A few years ago, as I was preparing a lecture on 'Living Truthfully', a question posed in our college philosophy class more than thirty years before suddenly popped into my mind: *Is it better to be an unhappy Socrates or a happy pig?*

When I was in college, I puzzled over this question and couldn't decide. However, at that moment, the answer came to me in a flash. Obviously, it is better for Socrates to be Socrates and for the pig to be a pig. Happy doesn't come into it.

Of course, if we come to be content to be ourselves, we may not get happiness, but we will find joy. I used to read all the teachings about how we need our difficult life events so that we can learn something, and groan, 'Oh no, not another lesson.' I thought of these life lessons as a moral imperative which would make me a better person, a Good Girl in a higher and higher dimension.

But I now understand that each time I take back a bit of truth into myself and live it, what I've gained is not a lesson but a better life. It feels better to be free to be myself. It is as simple as that.

14

Beyond Noah's Ark
Open up to a Soul Community

When burnout brings us to the edge of our known world, it can feel profoundly lonely. Yet who can we bring with us when we stand on the edge? Who will take our hand but not stop us from facing our truth in that place of aloneness we all need to know and go to? And when we have faced our fears and begun a new life, what will we hold on to, as we once held on to security and identity and roles and money and knowledge?

This chapter addresses the question: Can I find company when I dare to challenge whatever it was that held together my old relationships at work or at home?

Previously we have been held like a pot-bound plant, whose shape is now the shape of the pot. Our container was made of second-hand principles, needs, expectations and demands which we swallowed whole from our families, our work-places, our reference groups. We listened to our mother or father and not our soul. We listened to our boss and not our soul. We listened to our partner and not our soul. We listened to our children and not our soul.

Now we want to be held the way the sea holds us, buoyant, afloat, but free. We need relationships that support our being and becoming. I would call these relationships a soul community.

Two by two is not the only way to stay afloat

Honouring the importance of community rather than just the pairs and the families and the work roles that we have relied upon until now can be a radical departure for many of us. Doris, accountant, was willing to do anything to avoid giving up the life of being in a couple. Sue Townsend asked herself, *Who am I without my writing? I am nothing.* Holding on in this way put us at risk. When the old forms aren't big enough for our new sense of self, we need something larger.

A story comes to mind of my own difficulty in letting go of smaller forms. I was sitting with my friend Geoff, and feeling irrationally angry at him just because he was a man and I wasn't feeling too good about men, having just broken up a relationship with a lover.

'Where were you when . . . ?' I began threateningly.

'Where was I when – in the war?' he wondered.

'No, in the Flood. When Noah was getting all those animals on his ark, two by two? How was I going to be saved from the flood if I wasn't in a pair?'

I told my friend Helen this story and she recently wrote to tell me that she is starting a café on Mount Ararat for anyone who didn't get on the Ark. This makes me smile as I write it. But it was such a powerful archetypal image that I knew it was more than a joke. On some unconscious level, two-by-two seemed to be the only way to stay afloat. Otherwise, I would not be saved.

It takes courage to let go of all our deeply held beliefs and open to a larger picture. Yet two-by-two or work or family cannot be the only way to stay afloat. We need them, yet we mustn't need them so much that we blind ourselves to our truth as we did when we began on the burnout trail.

We yearn to feel welcomed and cherished while we wait, give up hope and keep the faith, work towards giving our soul a good home, and reach towards more honesty. We can do this in a soul community.

The communities we escaped from

Not every community is a soul community. The old-style communities that were once the norm were not. They held us, but didn't give our soul breathing room.

When we mourn the loss of the old communities, as we so often do, we don't always remember how many of the people who live in cities have voluntarily escaped from such communities. True, these communities gave us a sense that we were known, cared for, and belonged. But we paid for this by having to fit into the roles that were predetermined for us, to take up our part in the chain of history. The main mechanism of social control was gossip. Everyone knew our business, and if they didn't like it – and gossip didn't put us in our place – there would be trouble.

Maya, the psychotherapist living in London, talked of how she used to yearn for her extended family in South America that she'd been 'yanked out of' as a child when she was sent to a British boarding school.

All these years I've been harping back to that community, feeling it was a kind of Latin Nirvana, feeling I was missing out. But I've finally realized that the cost was too high. It's so great there in a way because you're in and out of each other's houses, laughing all the time, and you're enveloped in this love and togetherness. But if you stray out you are judged. I couldn't live that way. Now I know why I am here.

Many people, particularly those of us who did not fit with the stereotypes and conventional roles of that community, needed the anonymity of the city. Anonymous was good because it gave us a chance to find our own path, to risk change without an audience. Who was listening and watching? Who was criticizing? No one the child in us recognized.

But again there was a price: alienation and loneliness. If there was no one to criticize, perhaps there was also no one to care. And who was there to give a welcoming smile as we went about our daily life? Many of us have people we personally know and love and feel loved by, but not a tribe, not the larger social world. We need our near and dear, but we also need our community.

From old relationships to soul community

What kind of community will nourish us? Particularly during that delicate healing time from burnout, when all we know is what we do not know, we need people who have no vested interest in who we used to be and what we might be finding out. We need a community which gives space for our soul.

Julie, arts organization director, told me:

> *During my healing I started making connections again. Those connections with my friends, my soulmates, have kept the embers alive when all I could do was taste ashes. They kept the faith when I couldn't see it. Without them, it would have been like living in isolation in a cold cell. I think I would have shrivelled and died. It would have been completely meaningless.*

Our soul community can include people we already know and love as well as new people. Which people? It is those who care for us unconditionally, honour what we are becoming and wish us to go as far on this path as we want to go. It helps if they are themselves committed to their own truth and development; otherwise there will be no-go areas which cannot be talked of or dealt with.

Soul friends will not be happy about everything we do. They won't want us to harm ourselves by stunting our growth, getting addicted, neglecting or deadening ourselves, or making ourselves ill. They will be supporting us to grow and flower.

How do we recognize them? We know them by how we feel in their presence. These are some questions we can ask ourselves to find out:

Do I feel completely myself with this person or group? Can I say anything I want to? Can I express my fear, my anger, my love freely? Do they want me to be happy in my own terms? (If so, they sound like candidates for your soul community.)

Are there implicit rules, taboos or assumptions that must not be challenged? Do I subtly go into some role with them? Do they wish I were how I used to be? Are they envious or competitive? Are they so impressed that they can't really see me? Do they rely emotionally on my old ways of being with them? Do they want what *they* want for me rather than what I want for me? (If so, not so good.)

Leila, retreat director, described how she recognized people and atmospheres that were good for her now:

The important thing seems to be that when I'm with that person or group, I have a good experience of being me. The fuller range of being open is possible. It is safe to be angry or just to be me. Looking back, I can see what a closed in space I lived in with the group I have left. I wasn't having good experiences being me.

Janey, health consultant and editor, described her growing soul community:

It's people I can be myself in my fullest sense with, people who are also self-aware, working on their own development, and trying to live in the now.

Jeff, counselling manager, told me:

I was in such a muddle, I really needed other people to help me to see the truth. What I needed was people who could see through the hero and value who I really am, not what I do, not what I achieve. I lost a lot of my friends, and they got reduced to those who were also on a soulful journey and really came from a deep loving place. They had no judgment about me and my illness. They might not have named it a soul thing but it was. Two communities which I found through doing courses also became important to me because they had that quality.

Please don't give up on people prematurely. People who have been in our lives may be used to the old rules, which we have ourselves colluded to create. If we are open with people, and say what we haven't dared to say, we may find that the response surprises us, and that together we can create a new kind of relationship. Mary, airline planner, spoke of this.

I'm determined to be more honest with my friends and particularly with my mother. I always felt the pressure from my mother to achieve and get the next promotion. But then she came straight out and said, 'I think you're doing the right thing. Good for you.' So having presented my real self and my real aspirations to her somewhat nervously, I was supported. And everyone I have spoken to honestly about it has been supportive and encouraging which has been wonderful.

The communication structures, *oekos* and *co-listening*, under Try This . . . below can help transform old work-places and relationships into soul communities. Structures that encourage open communication can also serve as a barometer to recognize relationships that feel too rigid. If you can't imagine talking to certain people or groups for three minutes without censoring yourself, they are probably not, or not yet, your soul community. If you can't imagine doing so with anyone, you need to start imagining better.

Soul communities galore

Soul communities include people and books and music and teachers and CDs and films. They include people all around the world with whom we communicate through e-mail, as well as friends who live near enough to drop in. They range from friendship groups to course participant networks to people we make music with. They include permanent or temporary communities that we may join for retreats or holidays or for more extended periods. Whatever and wherever they are, they will have an atmosphere that supports us in our truth, nourishes our soul, and gives a hint of freedom.

Carl, whose story was told in Chapter 1, became interested in a community building network, which he first joined and then helped facilitate.

I got to know new people and I found a way of relating where I could safely look into myself. The community gave a context in which I could find a language, discover new relationships and explore who am I – what's my identity, what it is to be a human being. I had to find a new identity.

Leila, opened up both to an international community she had e-mail contact with and to her existing local community.

> *I have contacts in Australia and Canada through e-mail that mean a lot to me. I'm conscious that there other people working in the world in similar ways, that we are one world. Locally I feel much more in touch with a wider range of people, through dancing and singing and ordinariness – going to the pub, and nattering after singing in the choir. Equally, I have some very close relationships with people nearby.*

Alice, singer and songwriter, felt that the group she was making music with was her soul community.

> *I really needed to sing, to keen: that's the old Irish tradition when you keen or sing away your woes. I found the right community to do that with whom I could play with, who would support me and encourage the kind of mourning through music that would get me through to the other side.*

All the burnout people I know found some way of opening up to a soul community, and/or transforming their existing friends and family and colleagues into one, though they might never have used such a word.

The Skyros community

My own first-hand experience in the power of community has grown out of the Skyros holiday communities which we set up in 1979. Skyros began in large part because I myself was so desperate for community. I was running weekend personal development work-shops, where the atmosphere of truth-telling and loving was inspiring, but when I went to my lecturing job on Monday morning, it felt as if just walking in the corridors made me shrink. And I had not yet found a tribe of people with whom I could communicate on a deep level. My yearning for a community where I could expand and laugh and be honest was overwhelming.

New communication structures

We normally think of a live-in community as a shared permanent home. Skyros is a permanent centre, yet the community is created again and again every two weeks by the participants and the staff who are there at the time. We consider it a 'symbolic community', one which provides a transformational experience of community that we can bring back into our everyday lives.

When we set up Skyros, we knew we needed to find ways to create a community atmosphere quickly, one in which everyone, including the staff, was learning and growing and had a sense of belonging. Most of us are are so fully socialized into an alienated culture that unless new communication rules are introduced very early on, honesty and intimacy with strangers feel embarrassing.

In a typical session at Skyros, we use a range of communication structures to help people let go of barriers, leave behind old social rules, and be able to be fully present within hours or at the most days. These – and a staff selected not only for their skills but for their qualities of authenticity and warmth – have been remarkably success-ful in creating a two-week soul community with warmth, safety, joy and challenge fairly consistently session after session for twenty-three years. While what we were doing was pioneering in the late 1970s, similar structures have emerged in networks around the world.

Here are some ingredients that you may like to consider for your own use. Some are for setting up a larger community or conference, while others can be introduced anywhere. They won't work without a positive commitment, particularly by the people who set the tone of the community, to be authentic and loving and willing to deal with whatever is coming up rather than sweeping things under the carpet. If you are creating a relatively large community, it also helps to have someone with a vision of the whole to hold the focus. This may be a rotating role.

These major building-blocks were in place from the first days of Skyros:

- *Demos*, the Greek word for 'the people', is like a daily town meeting and oral newspaper for the whole community. There are also longer community meetings in the beginning, middle and end of each session. *Demos* gives participants the direct experience of having a say in the life of their community, rather than being passive guests.

- Work groups, where people spend about half an hour a day together cutting vegetables or sweeping or watering the garden, similarly encourage a group sense of responsibility and contribution.
- Courses which aim at developing the whole person and at creating intimate spaces are the centrepiece of the day. There is a sufficiently wide variety to enable each person to go to their growing edge, whether it be by windsurfing, ceramics or a relationships group.
- Social activities, often impromptu, and creative performances and cabarets, expand the joy and the shared creativity.
- The underlying ethos includes principles like 'being yourself in the presence of another', taking risks, being caring yet honest. They are a reminder that love, truth and freedom need to come together.

A structure that emerged at Atsitsa, the largest of our communities, is called *oekos*, the Greek word for 'home'. *Oekos* is a home group of about eight people that meets daily. It is an opportunity to take turns speaking spontaneously for a few minutes each and to be listened to by the group. Everyone at Atsitsa, from participants to teaching staff to permanent staff, does *oekos*. Staff meetings at all the centres begin with a brief *oekos*. When we had gatherings in London to consider how best to bring a Skyros atmosphere into everyday life, this emerged as the most portable and powerful way to do it. There are now *oekos* groups in various places around the world.

A similar form of talking and listening is co-listening, which happens in pairs. This has also travelled the world, deepened a lot of relationships, and given people a forum to be present to themselves and each other. Instructions for both *oekos* and co-listening are given under Try This . . . below. If you know similar structures that you are comfortable with, do of course use those.

Simple and safe communication structures such as these open up the possibility for what I call 'real talk' and 'real listening'. Real talk happens when we wait, open a space, and find out what comes up, instead of planning our story in advance or censoring ourselves. This sense of trust in ourselves and in our listener is one that few of us experience in everyday life. Real listening happens when we are fully present to another, resisting any temptation to help by interrupting, rescuing, constructively criticizing, interpreting or giving advice. Even a few minutes of real talk and real listening can create profound intimacy and enable us to find our own way through feelings and problems that seemed insoluble before.

Another level of communication which is crucial in a soul community is that with ourselves. Spending a little time on our own each day integrating what is happening, and listening to our own soul, is vital if we don't want to get lost again in other people's voices, even people we like and trust.

Each of these building-blocks lends another layer to the community atmosphere. If we were starting Skyros now, I would probably want to include some form of community meditation as well.

Recently I met someone, now a psychotherapist, whose stay in Skyros in one of the early years had changed her life. She told me that what had turned her life around was the combination of laughing all the time and of finding she could value herself during a period when she was a single mother and housewife without much education and with no self-esteem. Her story, like so many I have heard, reminded me of the power of an authentic and joyful soul community.

Coming home

When major life change happens in Skyros and other temporary soul communities, as it does for so many people, it needs to be supported and maintained back home. We need bridges between the short-term world of a holiday or retreat and the long-term way we live our lives. One of these bridges is continuing contact with the people with whom we have the kind of deep connection that is forged in a soul community. Such a bank of people holds us at that delicate moment when we are peeping out from the chaos of not-knowing into new ways of being.

Accompanied within as well as without

A soul community is not just in the external world. We also need an inner community. This can include our images of friends or family, memory pictures of family members who have died, spiritual beings, mythic heroes and heroines, inspiring historic figures, wise teachers, people who are working in a similar direction to us, or any image we have that represents the soul qualities we need. When we are feeling lonely or lost or in pain, it is good to call up these people or beings or images to love or guide us. The exercise *A circle of love* under Try This . . . below is one way to do this.

Thich Nhat Hanh (Thay) spoke to us of how when he is troubled by memories in his body from all the years of the Vietnam war, he would imagine he was lying in the arms of the Bhodisattva, God/Goddess of Love and Mercy, and fall asleep that way.

Our inner community is particularly vital during recovery from burnout. When we are in transition between an old way of life and a new one, we often feel anxious, lost or ungrounded. Rather like taking a plane trip to a new place, and not yet feeling we've arrived, we are suffering a kind of 'jet-lag of the soul'. It takes time to reform in our new world. At such a time our inner community reminds us who we are, and that we are always accompanied, both within and without.

Carina, consultant, said of her slow path of recovery from burnout:

> *I didn't feel as if I could face big things. I held on to small things, like the realization in an intensive Spanish class that here at least was something I found quite effortless, and a burgeoning relationship with someone I could be myself with, and a wise and loving being in our Imagework group garden who just said 'You'll be all right.'*

When burnout challenges every identity we held dear, we can call in our inner as well as our outer community. Who am I now? I am he or she who is loved and known.

What do I do when I can't save the world singlehandly?

Eventually, we need communities not only to hold us, but to serve as a
focus for our creative understandings and contributions. Superman or
Superwoman has now vanished from the stage. There has to be
another way.

Carol, health consultant, who had burnt out when her programme
became very successful and she didn't get help, told me of an
extraordinary experience that forced her to change her do-it-all-
yourself attitude. Carol is very down-to-earth and has always dis-
trusted anything 'airy-fairy', so it was all a shock to her:

*One of the things that happened and this probably fits into the airy-
fairy in my life was this: I teach breath therapy so it's been part of
my personal practice to do my own sessions. It's my meditation. I
was having a session one morning and the breath grabbed me and it
started to breathe me in such a strong way that at first I felt really
anxious, and then I allowed myself to relax and surrender.*

*I started hearing this voice inside saying: 'This programme
doesn't belong to you.' And I remember thinking, 'I know that,
but my name is on the manual.' I was told that the reason I was
getting sick was that I couldn't hold the energy any more. It was
bigger than me, bigger than one person could hold. It was time for me
to let others come in. I was told to do certain things and to call
certain people and tell them to come to my advanced training.*

*And I'm sitting there and saying, 'I can't do that, I don't do hard
sell.' It drew me into this deep emotional process. But I was told to do
these things and watch and listen and pay attention to what
happened. I thought people would think I was crazy and maybe
I am crazy. The session took about an hour and then I cried for three
hours. I didn't want to do it and didn't know what was happening
to me.*

*I called one person who is usually my touchstone. She said, 'So let
me tell you what happened to me today.' She had had an experience
where she was told that she should call me and say she wanted to go
on the advanced training and that she should work with me. She*

had pulled over on to the side of the road and cried. She was feeling that she couldn't tell me that because it was so presumptuous. It happened at the same time as my experience. And three or four other people had the same experience.

This coming together of inner messages created a remarkable trust between these people as to how to negotiate the path ahead.

Whether or not our experience is as rich in synchronicity as Carol's, we can all still open to a new way of living and working. We need to find a form that allows us to be part of something larger than ourselves. This doesn't mean we will physically work with others, but there will be some way in which we focus our energy or understanding to create a whole that is greater than the sum of its parts.

The metaphor of the goose with the golden eggs, which we looked at in Chapter 7, can take on a new lease of life here. Killing the goose for the golden eggs happened because greed over-reached itself. Taking care of the goose rather than its golden eggs is the lesson of burnout. Now another quality of the goose can take us to a new level: the way it cooperates with others.[1]

- As each goose flaps its wings, it creates an uplift for the birds following it. By flying in V-formation, the whole flock adds 71 per cent greater flying range than if a bird flew alone.
- Whenever a goose falls out of formation, it suddenly feels the drag and resistance of trying to fly alone and quickly gets back into formation to take advantage of the lifting power of the bird immediately in front.
- When the lead goose gets tired, it rotates back into formation and another goose flies at the point position.
- The geese in formation honk from behind to encourage those in front to keep up their speed.
- When a goose gets sick or wounded or shot down, two geese drop out of formation and follow it down to help and protect it. They stay with it until it is able to fly again or it dies. Then they launch out on their own with another formation to catch up with the flock.

We can no longer singlehandedly save the world. But then we are no longer singlehanded. We are part of a working, living, transforming whole.

Try This: A circle of love and/or Oekos and/or Co-listening

A circle of love

Who is there in your inner and outer life whom you would trust at a moment when you don't know who you are or where you are going and want to find out? Imagine these people and beings surrounding you in a circle of love and understanding. Feel their love for you healing you. Breathe in their love and breathe out your love to them. You can call up this circle whenever you feel threatened or alone or ungrounded. You can also choose any one person or being – a friend, perhaps, or your grandmother who especially loved and understood you, or God – and breathe in their love for a few moments every day.

Oekos

Checking in: A brief check-in is invaluable at the beginning of any meeting or gathering, particularly one where you feel there is no time for such things. It lets everyone settle into themselves, clear their energy and be free to focus on the task in hand. It is also a way to begin to turn work and work-places into soul community. This is a simple way to do it:

- Someone holds the focus for the meeting, and then people take turns speaking for about three minutes about whatever is on their mind and in their heart while everyone else listens silently, unconditionally open to whatever emerges. The idea is to speak without preparation. We 'open a space' and wait and see what emerges, a kind of thinking out loud in the presence of others. If we go blank during our turn, we still get our time. It often happens that after a silence something really important emerges.
- Then the meeting proceeds normally.

Oekos on its own: Consider whom you could have an *oekos* with, either among people you know or by spreading this idea among networks of people you are beginning to open up to. The www.skyros.com guestbook page is a place to let people know you are interested in *oekos* or to find someone else in your neighbourhood who is. This more extended *oekos* can also be introduced into work, or a conference you are organizing, or at the beginning of each day of a course, or your family.

- Use the above instructions for a check-in which can be more than three minutes each, depending on how much time you have. However, giving equal time to each person is important. Do have someone to hold the focus, keep timing clear, and make sure the discussion doesn't go off track. Each time you hold an *oekos*, a different member can play the role of facilitator.

- Before each person speaks, the 'facilitator' invites people to focus or tune in to themselves. Some people like to use a special object like a stone to pass around and hold when they talk. After each turn, the group may spend a moment imagining sending 'love' or 'light' or 'the best of everything' to the speaker.

- After everyone has had a turn, you can share what you feel and what themes have emerged. There are restrictions: no interpretation, no advice, no rescuing and no criticism.

- If you are with people you fully trust and you want to go deeper, you can do another round in which everyone starts off the sentence: 'And what I haven't told you is . . .' and wait to see what emerges to end this sentence. The next round can be: 'And what I haven't told myself is . . .' Do this a few times and you may find yourself going into places you haven't visited for a long time.

Co-listening: Co-listening has the same format of talking, listening, and sharing as *oekos* but is with only one other person.

- Choose one person whom you trust. It's best to do it with someone you can meet in person, but it is also possible on the phone. This can also be a wonderful way to deepen trust and open up your relationship with an intimate partner or spouse.
- The general pattern is that one talks while the other listens without saying anything, the listener then gives feedback, and then you switch.
- Each person takes ten or fifteen minutes, or some other agreed time, to talk and to be listened to. Again, each takes the time to 'open a space' and see what comes out, just thinking aloud. Try it at least once with your eyes closed to see if that works better for you. If you go blank, just wait and see what comes up. The listener can send love or warmth at the end of a talking period.
- When you're listening, you may like to experiment with imagining that you are sitting in a cone of light shining down from above. This helps to keep you in a good space and to hear what is beyond the surface words.
- The important thing is not how much time you each take but that it is equal time: some of us are so used to putting ourselves last that this needs to be firmly in the rule-book.
- Feedback can happen after each talk period, or after both are over. This needs to be timed or it could go on for ever – five or ten minutes is usually enough. As in *oekos*, there is no interpretation, no advice, no rescuing and no criticism. You can share how you felt about what the other said, or reflect back in brief what you heard the person saying. If you do reflect back, you need to check that the other person experiences it as accurate. If not, let them have the last word.

Finally: Belonging

Many of us burnout people have spent our lives honing our individualism. We feel like outsiders in many of the social structures around us, and may be suspicious of the very notion of belonging. The principles of the institutions we know may be antithetical to our own and there is often not much we can do about it.

These institutions are like solid structures which we may walk in and out of, voting with our feet if we are not happy. They are essentially indifferent to our coming and going.

A soul community has walls made up of people. Each time we move, we create a new shape. We matter. The delight of a soul community is that we can finally be part of a world that values our individuality as well as our connectedness. It honours who we really are, no matter what that may be.

15

From Wholeheartedness to Wholeness
When the Way Opens, Don't Leave Your Joy Behind

We began this story wholehearted about what we were doing. Then we lost heart and went through a 'dark night of the soul'. All the cracks in our old way of working became a chasm, and we were divided against ourselves. Now we are moving, not backwards to wholeheartedness but forwards to wholeness. We are committed to being aligned not only with respect to our work or our relationships but to all of our being. This is what our joy is all about – being wholly who we are. What all those spiritual books say is true. Sometimes it takes a big plank of wood like burnout to get us to see it.

This final chapter explores the questions: What has changed? Do we have more joy? Can we bring that joy which we found in tranquillity back into the world?

For most burnout people, much has changed and there is a new kind of joy. But we need to be able to walk slowly and mindfully into the future, with our whole self present and our connections to our soul community intact. We may not see very far ahead, but as long as the light illuminates our next step, we are safe. Not knowing doesn't threaten us in the same way. We will find out when the time comes.

Now our concern is not so much with dreams coming true as with being true to our dreams. And most importantly: knowing what our true dreams are.

So what was it all about?

As we emerge from burnout, it is good to look back and see where it brought us. What was it all about? Each of us needs to formulate this for ourselves, and to remind ourselves of it if we start to lose the plot. When I asked people what burnout meant to them, these were a few of the responses:

> *It was a feeling of opening out and a chance to see things differently, to live differently – without effort, without struggle, without anxiety.*
>
> Gemma

> *It's made me mindful that I need to take care of me first and everything else comes out of that. That's been a major shift. If I don't do the things that are important to me, like just being in my garden, my life will be out of balance.*
>
> *It has meant going into the pits to such a degree that the only alternative is a fundamental reappraisal of values held dear. Without that, I might never have climbed back out of the pit. I could have become alienated from my family and they might not have forgiven me. So it's been a period of growth which has continued even after the burnout was over.*
>
> Jack

> *Burnout enabled me to surrender to the bad feelings and the hurt and the horrible truth, the stuff I didn't want to see, and then to find the honesty and truth and look forward. The beauty of it is that you don't end up the same person as before.*
>
> Mary

> *It's meant the development of a spiritual path. Some of my ego got burnt out – the shoulds and the oughts and the control. I don't think the real part of you gets burnt out. You need your ego but there are times when it gets too strong and overshadows the soul and tries to control it. I think that's why burnout happens – for the soul to shine through.*
>
> Judith

Having recovered and come out the other end has meant a tremendous feeling of achievement because I've understood myself better and also have a bigger picture of the whole of life. It's made me aware of the fullness of my being. It's made me a whole person.

Cara

My purpose is now to heal myself – to acknowledge my true self and heal my false self – and to support others to grow to be themselves. Perhaps without burnout, I would not have found the path that was right for me. I am grateful and feel blessed.

Margaret

It has made me aware of all aspects of myself. I'd say I was a car only using two gears before and I wore those two gears out and found that I have another set of gears that is fresh and ready to go. It's to do with that sense of discovering the person I am and really being with people. And also taking responsibility and not running away from things, not using those false mechanisms like alcohol that I used to use. I was living in a small capsule and now I'm living in a big world.

Phil

When I asked Phil if he was glad he'd burnt out given the fact that he was still suffering from physical symptoms of chronic fatigue, he said:

Rather perversely I'd have to say yes. It was hell. You need the hell.

Our emerging joy

For most burnout people, joy was one of the great rewards of having gone through burnout and healed. Though they sometimes struggled for words in trying to explain what their joy was about, they fairly consistently described it as the result of having let go of old ways of worrying, controlling and driving themselves, and having begun to enjoy just being themselves, doing the simple things in life, and feeling more whole and more integrated. Jeff, counselling manager, worried about how clichéd he sounded when he described his joy:

It's a simple joy in a simple life, just getting up and having a cup of tea. Just going into the garden and touching a flower. It sounds clichéd. It is the joy of not being invested in how things turn out, not worried about what happened yesterday or will happen tomorrow. It's a very now-centred joy. And it doesn't really matter what anyone thinks of you.

Carina, consultant, described it this way:

I've always had a tendency to be a bit perfectionist, but I've realized that life's a bit short to wait until I can do things properly, so I'd better just have a bash at them in the meantime and see how things turn out. A lot of the things I used to get agitated about don't matter any more. I wake up naturally, feeling happy.

Kelly, a former social worker now doing local community organizing, said:

When I had joy before, it was more like a roller-coaster with joy at the peak of life. Now it feels more even and more grounded. It's something about going with the flow and the flow is where I'm going and it's at the right speed, and it feels good.

Edward, formerly an engineer, now an international workshop leader, told me:

The joy is in feeling fulfilled, in every day being different and in my understanding myself, valuing myself. I'm who I'm meant to be. The way I live my life is integrated. I'm not one person for my job and another person for my home and another person socially. I'm a unified person. I'm in a relationship which is like something I might have dreamed about and seen as an ideal as a teenager and looked at through rose-coloured glasses. My relationship, my work, my whole life are about exploring who I am and enjoying it. I'm not a different person but I'm who I am.

Janey, health consultant, told this story about her emerging joy which sums up much of what underlies this new post-burnout joy:

I was with my nephew who was three months old and I was flying this kite for the first time with him in a sling on my arm. I'm there in the moment, my senses are all awake. I'm feeling the wonderful warmth and heaviness of this sleeping baby, aware of this amazing trust that he could sleep on my breast and at the same time I am flying the kite so gently that I don't wake him.

And that is how you have to fly a kite anyway. It isn't straining after flying the kite, it just takes the lightest touch to keep that kite flying. We always think we have to strain and put in all this effort and actually the energy is there and it's just that light hand on the tiller. And there's also that wonderful wind and the sea and learning something new without having to set out to learn it. And at that moment I'm thinking – this is as happy as I'll ever be, it's wonderful.

Regressing

As we begin to think about the future, there is a tendency to regress. We've gone through this whole process, we've listened to ourselves, we've remembered who we are, we've started to create a new life and to find our joy. All good, all positive. And as usual, that in us which is lagging behind this process will kick up a fuss and demand to be paid attention to. We may start having a recurrence of old symptoms, old attitudes, old wounds. We may feel as if nothing has ever changed, in fact it is worse than ever.

We will doubt that the path we are choosing is right, particularly if it is very different from our old identities and from the culturally acceptable norm of how it is to be successful. When we find those doubts coming back, we need to do as we always do with Radical Healing – let go of whatever we are trying to hold on to. All the beliefs we have accumulated that we are doubting now have to go. Anything that stands in the way of our joy has to go too.

Dwell off the map for a while. Reconnect to how it feels to be you, to what you know indisputably because it is your body, your physical experience, the colours around you. And in reconnecting, find out what you know is so, because it is real.

Remember that Radical Healing is always about letting the darkness you are struggling with become the light that shows you the way.

- When you are hopeless, give up hope.
- When you are humiliated, let go of pride and choose humility.
- When you are disillusioned, de-illusion.
- When you are holding on to what you know, let go and surrender to what is about to become.

Do a mental checklist. Have I stopped listening? Stopped caring for myself? Stopped being honest with myself? Closed down from others? Begun to hold on to something? Have I forgotten whatever burnout was about for me? What is important? What is not important? Where is my joy now? What do I need to let go of to get it back? Go through the Radical Healing steps and recommit.

It also helps to go back to the *Control mind, heart, and soul* exercise in Try This . . . in Chapter 8, find out what your soul is whispering, and then step back into the light of the soul and identify with it. Then you can see all the doubts and fears for what they are, and sense what is deeper and more lasting. If this is hard to do, try just saying, 'I ask to come from my strength and not my weakness.'

When you're breathing easy, then and only then is it safe to venture out again. And don't hold your breath until whatever you are about to do gets done. Your breathing comes first. What you do is what you do.

Just as you start to go back into life, it is good to remind yourself: *This is my new life*. And breathe. And smile.

Coming full circle

Burnout, that hard teacher, doesn't stop when it has given us a really tough test. We often get the same test again to see if we've learnt it this time. Many people who have burnt out find that they meet a similar situation to that which led to their burnout, and feel they are being challenged to see if they can do it differently now.

Doris, the accountant who burnt out and became very ill through rescuing her partner who had lost his job, was faced with precisely the same situation when he became unemployed once again. This time, however, she decided to do something different.

> *What happened on a subconscious level then is what happens consciously now. I'm saying that whatever he does with respect to a job is up to him. I'm not going to provide him with support to get a job. I'm not providing him with unlimited emotional support either. He's got to sort it out for himself this time because it is his problem and it is not my problem.*

Doris is learning to say the Great No to rescuing her partner – and at the same time a Great Yes to her own health and to the possibility of a relationship in which she can give and receive in a balanced way.

Carina, the consultant who burnt out after a change in the company she worked for, is also facing a similar situation again. She wrote to me:

> *My work situation could be seen as having come full circle in some ways. The company was taken over about two years ago, and now the parent company is itself about to be taken over by an even bigger group. I recognize some of the unreality of the way things are managed and (not) communicated, and the feeling that the match between my core skills and the company's centre of gravity is lessening. I'll almost certainly want to move on again when I've completed my Masters, if not before. Nor do I really know where I'll move to.*
>
> *My response is different though; perhaps it's precisely because I recognize the feelings, or because my strongest reference points lie*

outside the company. I still work very hard, but I'm less easily fazed by people who try to hook you in to accept unreasonable demands. I feel calmer about making it clear I won't absorb unlimited heat. I don't always get it right, needless to say.

Judith, management consultant, talked of her key to preventing burnout again.

I now see that burnout is about letting go and letting some aspects of life die and see what emerges in the ashes afterwards. So what I've learnt to do is to say: 'This is a potential burnout and I need to take care and let go and be aware of letting in.'

James, after burning out as a high flying marketing consultant, is now a successful entrepreneur. He is faced with many of his old pressures and some new ones, but he is able to stay more centred. He told me:

You don't have to give everything up after burnout. You can go back into the business world and be a success. But what you do need to give up on is getting your identity or your self-esteem from your work success.

The challenge from life also comes in small ways every day. Once we have burnt out, burnout is always our teacher because we become more and more sensitive to those moments when we abandon our soul and succumb to our control mind. Life will never be the same again. But then, we wouldn't want it to be.

The way forward

Once we have found our feet, which means to say reconnected with our bodies and with the ground we walk on, we begin to find that we have new energy. This is a moment for caution. This new energy may be just a small burst that we take as a sign of spring but which is in reality just one swallow heralding the coming of spring. If we try to move at great speed immediately, we will soon find that our energy pockets are empty again.

The new energy that comes at first is for the small things that have come to matter to us. It is a gift from our whole being, and a promise, and it brings us joy. But it is not enough of a permanent legacy to create with.

Eventually, if we are patient enough, we start to get a sense that some more basic energy is coming back that is asking to be harnessed to our creativity. It is only at that point that we should consider having visions of the future, and wondering how to get there. It is now time to poke around in the ashes to rekindle the fire. But this time we need a new kind of fuel that is connected with who we are and not what we do and give. The process of healing is also the royal road into the future.

Sometimes, as we start to step forward, the world seems to step forward to meet us. We have that experience of 'the opening of the way' when strange coincidences happen, people we meet give us the nugget of information we need, just the right job comes along. This can restore our trust in life at moments when we wonder how we are going to find our way.

We cannot predict exactly what form our transformation will take. I have noticed that burnout people have created good lives, with successful and creative work which is important to us but not our whole story, with honest relationships, and with an enduring underlying sense of being at peace with ourselves.

We can still meet those deadlines if we want to, but we are more discerning about when to pull out the stops – and what level of excellence is good enough. We no longer feel that the results are all. We honour what we do, why and how we do it, and whether we keep to our own commitments. We are less dependent on knowing whom it impresses and whether or not it saves the world. The end results will emerge as and when they do. They are not under our control.[1] As a result, we have a new kind of authority about us – the authority of the heart.

Some of us have kept the same jobs or the same profession. Many have changed, not always in an obvious direction – except for a general trend toward being self-employed. The marketing manager has become an entrepreneur. The manager has become a coach of managers. The teacher is on the staff of a healing centre and has a private practice. The psychotherapist with a private practice is a writer. The geophysicist is a hypnotherapist. The drug addiction worker is a web designer.

When I say that the manager has become a coach, or any other form of X has become Y, it is a manner of speaking, the old way of speaking. The way we experience it is actually: 'We used to *be* X and now we are *doing* Y.' The ex-manager coaches managers. The ex-drug addiction worker does web design. We are not identified with our jobs any more. That is not where our value lies.

Some burnout people are just opening a space and not deciding too much. Leila, retreat director, is going off to Canada for six months to join a community she has been corresponding with by e-mail. What will she do? She doesn't know. That will emerge.

The people of burnout

We are taking our first groping steps. We are beginning to think it is possible to live truthfully as part of a world that makes sense, to love and be loved, to be creative and to make a difference. We are reaching out towards new understandings of how to do this, but we are often forced back on old models, on old ways of earning our daily bread and of being of value.

The next step, I believe, is to connect to that vast and ever-increasing group of creative people who are becoming free to find new ways to create and contribute. This can become a reservoir for a new form of living and of giving to the community and society we are part of.

My hope is that this book will be part of a process whereby people who have burnt out will get to know each other, share experiences and find out how their lives and creativity might follow a common pathway. I encourage you to go to www.skyros.com Burnout page and leave a message or a plan in the guest-book or respond to someone else's message or plan. That could be a beginning.

I believe that the people of burnout can pioneer a profound change in consciousness and in our present social structures. When we burnt out, it was to do with where and how we invested our creativity and our belonging. We became unable to continue in the old structures and needed to find another way forward by going deep into our true selves. Many of us will now want to find new ways to create and belong, not just for ourselves but for others, and link up with networks around the world who are doing something similar.

We who have been through burnout will have some idea about which environments are life-enhancing and which are soul-destroying. We will know what it takes to listen to our soul, and how easy it is to ignore the whispers and go with the roars of the crowd around us. We will have the desire to create around us environments which support other people in their being and becoming. We are aware from our own hard experience that if people do what is not right for them, what they do will not bear the right kind of fruit.

We may well begin to wonder how we can create the perfect environment. As we get into our old perfectionism, we will fail and then we will be discouraged. But then, hopefully, we will reach out to others for help instead of getting up and dusting ourselves off and going it alone.

We will not create a perfect environment, nor a perfect soul community, nor a perfect world. We will only create perfect opportunities for all of us to keep building up our 'living truthfully muscle'.

Try This: The way forward

So how do we find the way forward? How do we start to vision where it is we want to go? A great deal has been written about this in the past few years, and my book *Life Choices, Life Changes* addresses this at length by offering ways to work with the imagination to find your vision and to carry it through. There are also many workshops and courses and lectures devoted to this subject. But here are a few questions and exercises tailored for burnout people:

A few questions

- *If I could wave a magic wand over my life, how would it be?* If that magic wand shows you relaxing on a beach and doing nothing, you are probably still in need of rest and healing.
- *When I think of using my creativity, do I just feel weighed down by the responsibility?* If you do, you probably need to spend more time looking at what attachments or investments you still have: to success, outcomes, getting it right, being a star or a hero or a perfect being.
- *Where is my joy? What do I need to do to keep it alive?* Even when you get a sense that the way forward could itself be joyful, you need to make sure that the doing won't crowd out those empty spaces.

Five steps back and six forward

This exercise can illuminate the theme of your life that is most relevant to you today and help you to get a sense of your next step. You can do it again and again – it will be different each time.

- Take five steps back in time and see where you land. Allow a memory picture to emerge of some time in the past. What is it?
- Now move forward one step at a time. As each foot reaches the ground, wait until some picture emerges of a time in your life or an experience. When you've taken five steps, you should be back at or near the present.
- Now take another step forward (into the future). What experience are you having now?
- If you want to, take one more step. Now what?
- Reflect.

From thought to intention

- If you have an idea of what you want to do next, ask yourself for an image of you in the future *after* you have done whatever you are considering doing. Step into that future picture. How do you walk? How do you feel? What is a day in your life like? Do you feel authentic and joyful? Look back and see how you got here – what steps you took, what difficulties you overcome.

- If you don't like what you find, it doesn't necessarily mean the idea is bad. It may mean that there is something about your image of it that doesn't work yet. Try asking for another image that is more consonant with who you really are.
- Once you have a plan or a picture of what you want and a sense of where you need to go to get there, check it out with:
  - *Your inner child*: Ask for an image of the child that you were, whichever age comes to mind. Talk together about your plans.
  - *Your House of Truth*: Go back to the House of Truth in Try This . . . in Chapter 13 and sit on the Throne of Truth. What is the truth about this plan?
  - *Your body*: Tune in to your body, or get an image of your body and talk to it. How does your body feel about the project, and what does it need from you? The exercise *Listening to my body* from Try This . . . in Chapter 8 is a good one.
  - *Your control mind, your heart and your soul*: Go back to this exercise in Try This . . . in Chapter 8. Your soul is probably the best adviser, and your control mind the worst.
  - *Your soul community*: Think of someone in your soul community whose judgment and love you trust. Ask them what they think of this new plan. Don't just take their advice. Listen carefully and then judge for yourself.

The bubble
- Once you know you are on the right path, step out of the picture, and do the Bubble exercise from Try This . . . in Chapter 12. Put that picture in a bubble, ask and intend for it to be, release it and let it fly off, and then bring the future feeling into your heart now and say *Thank you. It is already so.*

Finally: What's new?

It is easy to find *a* way forward. We burn-out people have a thousand ideas and all of them are good. But they may not be good for us.

Before, we were able to follow a vision of what needed doing, while leaving the slower bits of us way behind. Never mind about our body, our heart, our emotions, our soul: they will catch up later, we reasoned, once we were securely 'there'. Now, we know that although they move slowly, they are way ahead of us and we need their wisdom and love. We can't go anywhere without all of us, nor is it safe to cut off from our soul community.

This is a slower way. Or so said the hare to the tortoise.

In some ways we will feel more alone, as we have to refer our choices to our own soul rather than merging with others. Yet we now have a community with which we can resonate and which supports our individuality as well as our connectedness. The outlines of where this aloneness and community can take us emerge day by day. We don't have our old certainty and yet we are safe.

Cooperating with burnout has brought us here. Now, our new way of living is beginning to show its full power and its most profound and lasting joy. When we burnt out we lost our way. Now we can't lose our way because we *are* the way and because 'we' really means 'we'.

The spiritual philosopher Krishnamurti,[2] when asked what the new world would be like, said, 'If I knew what it would be like it wouldn't be new.'

May we be surprised.

Notes and References

ACKNOWLEDGMENTS
1. 'Burnout people' or 'people of burnout' are my shorthand for people who have been through burnout and beyond.

CHAPTER 1: THE HIDDEN MESSAGE OF BURNOUT
1. Glouberman, Dina, *Life Choices, Life Changes: Develop Your Personal Vision with Imagework* (London: Thorsons, 1995) (first published by Unwin Hyman, 1989).
2. St John of the Cross, *The Dark Night of the Soul* (Cambridge, England: James Clarke & Co. Ltd, 1973).
3. Mann, Thomas, *Buddenbrooks* (NY: Alfred A. Knopf, 1924) (first published Berlin: Fischer Verlag, 1901).
4. Greene, Graham, *A Burnt-out Case* (NY: Vintage, 2001).
5. Freudenberger, H. J. and G. Richelson, *Burnout: The High Cost of High Achievement* (NY: Anchor Press, 1980), Freudenberger, H. J. and Gail North, *Women's Burnout: How to Spot It, How to Reverse It and How to Prevent It* (NY: Penguin Books, 1986).
6. Maslach, Christina, *Burnout: The Cost of Caring* (NJ: Prentice Hall, 1982); Maslach, C. and M. P. Leiter, *The Truth about Burnout* (San Francisco: Jossey Bass, 1997); Maslach, C., W. B. Schaufeli and M. B. Leiter, Job Burnout, *Annual Review of Psychology* (2001, 52: 397–422); Maslach, C. and W. B. Schaufeli, Historical and Conceptual Development of Burnout, in *Professional Burnout: Recent Developments in Theory and Research*, ed. W. B. Schaufeli, C. Maslach and T. Marek (London: Taylor and Francis, 1993); Maslach, C., S. E. Jackson and M. B. Leiter, *Maslach Burnout Inventory Manual*, 2nd. edn (California: Consulting Psychologists Press, 1996).

7. For example: Pines, A., *Keeping the Spark Alive: Preventing Burnout in Love and Marriage* (NY: St Martins Press, 1988).

8. These are a few of the more seminal references upon which this thumbnail sketch is based. They are, along with those listed above, a good starting-point for those readers who would like to be better acquainted with the research in the field: Burke, R. J. and A. M. Richardson, Psychological Burnout in Organizations, in *Handbook of Organizational Psychology*, ed. R. T. Golembiewski (USA: Marcel Dekkur, 2000); Cherniss, C., *Professional Burnout in Human Service Organizations* (NY: Praeger, 1980); Farber, B. A., ed., *Stress and Burnout in the Human Service Professions* (NY: Pergamon Press, 1983); Golembiewski, R. T. and R. I. Munzenrider, *Phases of Burnout: Developments in Concepts and Applications* (NY: Praeger, 1988); Golembiewski, R. T., R. Boudreau, R. Munzenrider and L. Huapino, *Global Burnout: a Worldwide Pandemic Explored by the Phase Model* (London: JAI Press, 1996); Pines, A. M., E. Aronson with D. Kafry, *Burnout: from Tedium to Personal Growth* (N.Y.: The Free Press, 1981); Pines, A. and E. Aronson, *Career Burnout: Causes and Cures*, 2nd edn (NY: Free Press, 1988); W. S. Paine, ed., *Job Stress and Burnout Research: Theory and Intervention Perspectives* (California: Sage, 1982); W. B., Schaufeli and Dirk Enzman, *The Burnout Companion to Study and Practice: A Critical Analysis* (London: Taylor and Francis, 1998); Schaufeli, W. B., C. Maslach and T. Marek, eds, *Professional Burnout: Recent Developments in Theory and Research* (London: Taylor and Francis, 1993).

CHAPTER 2: DON'T TAKE IT TOO PERSONALLY

1. Handy, C., *The Search For Meaning* (London: Lemos and Crane, 1996); Handy, C., *The Elephant and the Flea: Looking Backward to the Future* (London: Hutchinson, 2001).

2. McGee-Cooper, A., D. Wilson and T. Chamberlain, Second Wind: Tools for Balancing Life with Work at Southwest Airlines (Cassette Recording), *The 2000 Systems Thinking in Action Conference* (Pegasus Communications, Inc., 2000).

3. Personal communication.

4. Drabble, Margaret, *Public Speech and Public Silence* (Gulbenkian Lecture Theatre, Oxford, 18 October, 2001).

5. Katzenberg, S. E., *I Want a Divorce?* (London: Kyle Cathie Ltd, 1999).

6. Sue Townsend's best-selling books include: *The Secret Diary of Adrian Mole Aged 13¼* (1982), *The Growing Pains of Adrian Mole (1984)*,

Rebuilding Coventry (1988) *True Confessions of Adrian Albert Mole, Margaret Hilda Roberts and Susan Lilian Townsend* (1989), *Adrian Mole: From Minor to Major* (1991), *The Queen and I* (1992), *Adrian Mole: The Wilderness Years* (1993) and *Ghost Children* (1998).

CHAPTER 3: ARE YOU BURNING OUT, BURNT OUT OR JUST PLAIN SICK AND TIRED?

1. According to Carolyn Myss's 'energy anatomy' system, typical burnout symptoms such as exhaustion, energy disorders and sensitivities to light are related to the 'seventh chakra' issues such as trusting life, values, humanitarianism, faith, seeing the larger picture and spirituality. See Myss, C., *Anatomy of the Spirit: The Seven Stages of Power and Healing* (London: Bantam, 1997).
2. Cavafy, C. P. *The Complete Poems of C. P. Cavafy*, translated by Rae Dalven with an introduction by W. H. Auden (London: Chatto and Windus, 1961).
3. Mann, Thomas, *Buddenbrooks* (NY: Alfred A. Knopf, 1924) (first published Berlin: Fischer Verlag, 1901).
4. Bennet, Glin, *The Wound and the Doctor* (London: Martin, Secker and Warburg, 1988). Bennet discusses how doctors burn out and continue without commitment.
5. Rumi. *The Essential Rumi*, translated by: Coleman Barks (London: Penguin Books, 1999) (first published NY: HarperCollins, 1995).

CHAPTER 4: WHEN WE WERE WHOLEHEARTED

1. For example: Timmen L. Cermak, *Diagnosing and Treating Co-dependence* (Minneapolis: Johnson Institute Books, 1986).
2. Childre, D. and H. Martin, *The HeartMath Solution* (USA: Institute of Heartmath, 2000).
3. Becker, E., *The Denial of Death* (NY, London: The Free Press, 1973).

CHAPTER 6: TRAPPED

1. *A Course in Miracles* (London: Arkana, 1985) (first published USA: Foundation for Inner Peace, 1975).
2. Wright, Chris, The Gambler, *Pacific Sun* (25 April, 2001), p. 14.
3. Gibran, Kahlil, *The Prophet* (London: Pan Books, 1991) (first published by William Heinemann, 1926). The original lines are: 'You may give them your love but not your thoughts, for they have their own thoughts' (p. 22).

4. There is a beautiful discussion on the importance of facing our abyss and our broken heart in intimate relationships in Welwood, John, *Love and Awakening: Discovering the Sacred Path of Intimate Relationship* (NY: HarperPerennial, 1997).

CHAPTER 7: NEARLY KILLING THE GOOSE THAT LAYS THE GOLDEN EGGS

1. For good discussions of this see: Schaef, Ann, Wilson Schaef and Diane Fassell, *The Addictive Organization* (San Francisco: Harper and Row, 1988); Maslach, C. and M. P. Leiter, *The Truth about Burnout* (San Francisco: Jossey Bass, 1997).
2. Miller, A., *The Drama of the Gifted Child* (London: Basic Books, 1982).
3. For a good discussion of this, see Lerner, H. G., *The Dance of Intimacy* (NY: Harper and Row, 1989).
4. Rubin, T. I., *Compassion and Self Hate: An Alternative to Despair* (NY: David McKay Company, 1975).

CHAPTER 8: WHEN SOMETHING IS MORE IMPORTANT THAN THE TRUTH

1. *I Ching or Book of Changes*, translated by Richard Wilhelm and rendered into English by C. F. Baynes, with a foreword by C. G. Jung (London: Arkana, 1989).

CHAPTER 9: BURNOUT AND BEYOND

1. I believe this is by Vernon Law.
2. Levinson, D. J., *The Seasons of a Man's Life* (NY: Alfred A. Knopf, 1978). 'De-illusionment' is Levinson's term for mid-life reality testing.
3. Glouberman, Dina, *Life Choices, Life Changes: Develop Your Personal Vision with Imagework* (first published by Unwin Hyman, 1989; available from Hodder & Stoughton from 2003); *Image Power – Inner Power tape series: Every Person's Guide to Life Choices and Changes*. Books and tapes, available individually or as a set of eight, can be ordered from the Skyros London office, contact details of which can be found at the back of this book.

CHAPTER 10: NO WAY FORWARD BUT TO STOP

1. Eliot, T. S., *Collected Poems 1909–1962* (London, Faber and Faber, 1936).
2. Dennis Palumbo writes about how burnt-out writers need to stop and rest in *Writing from the Inside Out* (NY: John Wiley and Sons, 2000).

3. Two of Thich Nhat Hanh's many wonderful books are *The Miracle of Mindfulness: A Manual on Meditation*, translated by Mobi Ho (Boston: Beacon Press, 1987); and *Peace is Every Step: The Path of Mindfulness in Everyday Life*, with a foreword by H. H. The Dalai Lama (London: Rider, 1995).
4. Eliot, *Collected Poems*.

CHAPTER 12: FROM HOVEL TO PALACE

1. Pronounced *hey-hal* with the second h being guttural.

CHAPTER 14: BEYOND NOAH'S ARK

1. These facts come from an Internet site. If they are not literally accurate, please take them as a metaphor.

CHAPTER 15: FROM WHOLEHEARTEDNESS TO WHOLENESS

1. There is a beautiful discussion about this in Ram Dass and Paul Gorman, *How Can I Help?* (London: Rider and Co. 1986).
2. *The Penguin Krishnamurti Reader*, compiled by Mary Lutyens (Harmondsworth: Penguin, 1970).

Contact Details

To contact Dina Glouberman, or to set up workshops or speaking engagements, or to leave messages on the Burnout web page, or to start or join an *Oekos* group, or to receive more information about courses around the world, holidays on the Greek island of Skyros and in Thailand, or Imagework practitioners who offer individual sessions or courses, or to order books and tapes by Dina Glouberman, including *The Joy of Burnout, Life Choices, Life Changes*, and the *Image Power–Inner Power* tape series, contact:

www.joyofburnout.com

Skyros, 92 Prince of Wales, London, NW5 3NE.
Tel: +44 (0)207 267 4424/ +44 (0)207 284 3065
Fax: +44(0)207 284 3063
e-mail: connect@skyros.com
www.skyros.com
(*Oekos* Guestbook and holiday details)
www.imagework.co.uk

Inner Ocean Publishing

*Expanding horizons
with books that
challenge the mind,
inspire the spirit,
and nourish the soul.*

We invite you to visit us at:
www.innerocean.com

Inner Ocean Publishing, Inc.
PO Box 1239, Makawao
Maui, HI 96768, USA
Email: info@innerocean.com